NAKAMA 1

Workbook/Laboratory Manual

NAKAMA 1

JAPANESE COMMUNICATION, CULTURE, CONTEXT

Workbook/Laboratory Manual

Yukiko Abe Hatasa

University of Iowa

Kazumi Hatasa

Purdue University

Houghton Mifflin Company
Boston   New York

Director, Modern Language Programs: E. Kristina Baer
Development Manager: Beth Kramer
Associate Sponsoring Editor: Hélène Hideko de Portu
Senior Manufacturing Coordinator: Priscilla J. Abreu
Marketing Manager: Patricia Fossi

Illustration by Graham Lee, Travis Kain, and Kazumi Hatasa

Printed in the U.S.A.

ISBN: 0-669-27585-9

18 19 20 - HS - 08 07 06

Contents

TO THE STUDENT

The workbook/laboratory manual accompanying *Nakama 1: Japanese Communication, Culture, Context* is designed to increase your accuracy in grammar usage and your knowledge of **kanji** and to help you develop basic listening comprehension and production skills in Japanese. The exercises and activities in the workbook/laboratory manual are divided into two sections. The workbook consists of grammar and written exercises, and the lab manual provides pronunciation, listening, and oral production exercises. The pages have been perforated so they can be handed in.

The first section of the workbook consists of supplementary grammar exercises to complement those in the text. This section also includes a number of exercises with personalized questions that enable you to practice more creatively the central grammar principles covered in each chapter. The grammar exercises in the workbook, like those in the textbook, are situation based and reinforce the basic vocabulary in the textbook. In addition, the second section of the workbook (**Kaku Renshū**) provides penmanship practice for new **kanji** and exercises that reinforce your usage of **kanji** when writing in Japanese.

The laboratory manual consists of two sections: Pronunciation and Spoken and Listening Activities. In the first section, you will hear the Essential Vocabulary presented at the end of each chapter in your textbook. While listening to the tape, you should look at your vocabulary list, for which the reference page in your textbook is provided, and repeat the items to familiarize yourself with the visual symbols and their sounds. The second section provides supplementary listening and oral production exercises to complement those in the text. The exercises include formation exercises, true/false and multiple-choice exercises, task-based listening activities, and personalized questions.

NAKAMA 1

Workbook/Laboratory Manual

WORKBOOK

だいにか　(Chapter 2)
あいさつと　じこしょうかい
(Greetings and Introductions)

I. Identifying someone or something, using ～は　～です

Imagine that you have a pen pal in Japan and that you have become [ ]ends with the following students in your Japanese class. Write a short description of [ ]h student to your
pen pal. You may use **hiragana** for the words written in **katakana**.

なまえ (Name)	～じん (Nationality)	Gender	～ねんせい (Year in school)	～んこう (Major)
ブラウン	アメリカじん	おとこ	いちねんせい	こうがく
キム	かんこくじん	おとこ	だいがくい　　い	けいざいがく
チョー	ちゅうごくじん	おんな	にねんせい	えいご
モネ	カナダじん	おとこ	よねんせ	アジアけんきゅう
スミス	オーストラリアじん	おんな	さんね　　い	ぶんがく

■ ブラウンさんは　アメリカじんです。　お[ ]の　ひとです。
いちねんせいです。せんこうは　こうがく　す。

1. キムさんは _____。　_____。

_____。[ ]こうは _____。

2. チョーさんは _____ _____。

_____。せんこうは _____。

3. モネさんは _____。 _____。

_____。せんこうは _____。

4. スミスさんは ＿＿＿＿＿＿＿＿＿＿＿＿。＿＿＿＿＿＿＿＿＿＿＿＿＿＿＿。

＿＿＿＿＿＿＿＿＿＿＿＿＿＿＿。せんこうは ＿＿＿＿＿＿＿＿＿＿＿＿。

Name _____ Class _____ Date _____

II. Asking はい／いいえ questions, using 〜は　〜ですか

A. Look at the chart on page 7. Using the pattern 〜は〜ですか, write a question using the cue given. Frame the question so that B can answer yes. You may use **hiragana** for the words written in **katakana**.

■ （アメリカじん） A: ブラウンさんは　アメリカじんですか。 B: ええ、そうです。

1. （ちゅうごくじん）　　　A: _____。
　　　　　　　　　　　　　　B: ええ、そうです。

2. （だいがくいんせい）　　A: _____。
　　　　　　　　　　　　　　B: ええ、そうです。

3. （オーストラリアじん）　A: _____。
　　　　　　　　　　　　　　B: ええ、そうです。

4. （いちねんせい）　　　　A: _____。
　　　　　　　　　　　　　　B: ええ、そうです。

5. （よねんせい）　　　　　A: _____。
　　　　　　　　　　　　　　B: ええ、そうです。

6. （カナダじん）　　　　　A: _____。
　　　　　　　　　　　　　　B: ええ、そうです。

B. Write your answer to each of the following questions about yourself using ええ、そうです or いいえ、そうじゃありません／いいえ、そうじゃないです.

■ だいがくせいですか。　→　ええ、そうです。

1. メキシコじんですか。　　　　　　　_____

2. せんこうは　フランスごですか。　　_____

3. いちねんせいですか。 　　　　　　_____

4. アメリカじんですか。 　　　　　　_____
（あめりか）

5. だいがくいんせいですか。 　　　　_____

6. さんねんせいですか。 　　　　　　_____

III. Recognizing the relationship between nouns with の

Imagine that you are writing to your Japanese pen pal about your friends from Japan.
Look at the chart below and write something about each student, following the example.

なまえ (Name)	だいがく (University)	～ねんせい (Year in school)	せんこう (Major)
やまだ	おおさかだいがく	さんねんせい	えいご
おおき	とうきょうだいがく	だいがくいんせい	こうがく
さとう	じょうとうだいがく	よねんせい	けいざいがく
たなか	きょうとだいがく	にねんせい	ぶんがく
いとう	にほんだいがく	いちねんせい	けいえいがく
はやし	なごやだいがく	だいがくいんせい	スペインご
すずき	わせだだいがく	さんねんせい	ちゅうごくご

■ やまださんは　おおさかだいがくの　さんねんせいです。
　やまださんの　せんこうは　えいごです。

1. おおきさんは _____

　_____

2. さとうさんは _____

　_____

3. たなかさんは _____

　_____

4. いとうさんは _____

_____

5. はやしさんは _____

_____

6. すずきさんは _____

_____

IV. Asking for personal information, using question words

A. Complete the following dialogue, using the appropriate question words.

■ A: <u>やまださんは　どこから　きましたか</u>。

　　 B: とうきょうから　きました。

A: あのう、　すみません。(1) _____。

B: やまだです。

A: はじめまして、わたしは　たなかです。　どうぞ　よろしく。

B: こちらこそ、どうぞ　よろしく。　たなかさんは　がくせいですか。

A: ええ、そうです。　やまださんは。

B: わたしも　がくせいです。　じょうとうだいがくの　さんねんせいです。

　　 (2) _____。

A: わたしの　だいがくは　きょうとだいがくです。　せんこうは　こうがく
　　 です。

　　 (3) _____。

B: アジアけんきゅうです。　(4) _____。

A: よねんせいです。

B: そうですか。　これからも　どうぞ　よろしく。

A: こちらこそ。

V. Listing and describing similarities, using と and も

Find people who have things in common with you, such as their major, year in school, and instructors. First complete each of the following sentences about yourself. Then write a sentence about someone else who is like you in that respect. Write the person's name in **hiragana** or **romaji** if you don't know how to write it in **katakana**. Finally, write one sentence that combines the first two sentences, using と.

■ わたしは <u>にほんごの　がくせいです。</u>
　<u>スミスさんも　にほんごの　がくせいです。</u>
　　す　み　す
　<u>わたしと　スミスさんは　にほんごの　がくせいです。</u>
　　　　　す　み　す

1. わたしは _____ねんせいです。

　_____

　_____

2. わたしの せんこうは _____です。

　_____

　_____

3. わたしの　だいがくは _____だいがくです。

　_____

　_____

4. わたしの　せんせいは _____せんせいです。

　_____

　_____

5. わたしは _____からきました。

_____

_____

そうごうれんしゅう (Integration)

Smith-san and Tanaka-san have just met each other at a party at the International Student Center at Westside University. Complete their conversation, using the information from the following chart.

なまえ (Name)	だいがく (University)	〜ねんせい (Year in school)	せんこう (Major)	〜からきました (Hometown)
たなか	じょうとうだいがく	さんねんせい	えいご	とうきょう
スミス	にほんだいがく	いちねんせい	えいご	シカゴ

たなか: はじめまして。 たなかです。 どうぞ よろしく。

スミス: _____。スミスです。_____。

たなか: スミスさんは がくせいですか。

スミス: _____、_____。にほんだいがくの

いちねんせいです。

たなか: そうですか。わたしは _____さんねんせいです。

せんこうは えいごです。

スミス: そうですか。_____えいごです。

_____。

たなか:　　とうきょうから　きました。　スミス^{すみす}さんは　どこから

　　　　　きましたか。

スミス^{すみす}:　　_____。

だいさんか　(Chapter 3)
にほんの　うち
(Japanese Houses)

I. Describing buildings and rooms, using adjective + noun

Write your answer to each of the following questions, using the adjectives listed in the following box.

> おおきい　ちいさい　あたらしい　ふるい　ひろい　せまい　あかるい
> たかい　いい　きれい(な)　しずか(な)　りっぱ(な)　すてき(な)　ゆうめい(な)

■　～さんの　だいがくは　どんな　だいがくですか。
　　<u>ちいさい　だいがくです</u>。

1.　～さんの　だいがくは　どんな　だいがくですか。

　　_____

2.　～さんの　にほんごの　せんせいは　どんな　せんせいですか。

　　_____

3.　～さんの　ともだちは　どんな　ひとですか。

　　_____

4.　～さんの　うちは　どんな　たてものですか。

　　_____

5.　～さんの　へやは　どんな　へやですか。

　　_____

II. Referring to places, things, and people, using この, その, あの, どの

Look at the drawing of a bedroom. Alice is sitting on the bed (location A), and Michiko is at location B. Complete the following conversation, using この, その, あの, どの.

アリス：　　みちこさん、___この___ へやは　みちこさんの

　　　　　　　へやですか。

みちこ：　　ええ、そうです。

アリス：　　とても　あかるいですね。あのう、_____ (1) ねこは

　　　　　　　みちこさんの　ねこですか。

みちこ：　　ええ、そうです。なまえは　ミーです。

アリス：　　かわいいですね。(It's cute, isn't it?)　_____ (2) いぬも

　　　　　　　みちこさんの　いぬですか。

みちこ：　　え？_____ (3) いぬですか。

　　　　　　　　　　Workbook: Chapter 3　　**21**

アリス：　　(pointing outside the window)　＿＿＿＿＿＿＿ (4) いぬですよ。

みちこ：　　ああ、＿＿＿＿＿＿＿ (5) いぬは　となりの　ひと (neighbor) の

　　　　　　いぬです。

アリス：　　そうですか。ところで (by the way)、みちこさん。

　　　　　　＿＿＿＿＿＿＿ (6) たんすは　とても　すてきですね。

　　　　　　アンティークですか。(Is it an antique?)

みちこ：　　ええ。おばあちゃん (grandmother) の　たんすです。

III. Describing the location of people and things using ～に　～が　あります／います and ここ, そこ, あそこ, どこ。

A. Write your answer to each of the following questions. If you want to use a foreign word, try to write it in **katakana**.

■　とうきょうには　なにが　ありますか。

　じょうとうだいがくが　あります。

1.　ニューヨーク(New York)には　どんな　たてものが　ありますか。
　　にゅ　よ　く

　　_____

2.　フロリダ (Florida) には　なにが　ありますか。
　　ふ　ろ　り　だ

　　_____

3.　とうきょうには　なにが　ありますか。

　　_____

4.　ちゅうごくには　なにが　いますか。

　　_____

5. パリには　なにが　ありますか。

_____

6. ワシントン DC (Washington, D.C.)には　ゆうめいな　ひとが　いますね。

だれが　いますか。

_____

B. Look at the following illustration. The person at location A is describing various objects inside and outside the room to the person at location B. Write a sentence about each of the following objects, using ここ, そこ, あそこ, and 〜に　〜が　あります／います.

■ でんわ　<u>ここに　でんわが　あります。</u>

1. ベッド　^{べっど}　_____

2. ふとん　_____

3. ほんだな　_____

4. いぬ　_____

5. とだな　_____

6. ねこ　_____

IV. Using location nouns: なか, そと, となり, よこ, ちかく, うしろ, まえ, うえ, した, みぎがわ, and ひだりがわ

Look at the following illustration. Complete the following description, using location nouns. Use your right and left as you look at the room.

この へやの みぎがわには おおきい ソファ(そふぁ)が あります。 ソファ(そふぁ)の

_____ (1) に えが あります。 ソファ(そふぁ)の _____ (2)

には いすが あります。いすの _____ (3) には とだなが

あります。そして、とだなの _____ (4) に まどが あります。

いすの _____ (5) には テーブルが あります。とだなの

_____ (6) には ウィスキー (whiskey)が あります。テレビの

_____ (7) には しゃしんが あります。

B. Write your description of the following room, using location nouns.

■ へやの みぎがわに おしいれが あります。

_____

_____

_____

_____

V. Using よ and ね

Fill in the blanks with either よ or ね.

■ A: やまださんは　がくせいです＿ね＿。

　　B: ええ、そうです。

1. A: やまださんの　へやは　とても　きれいです＿＿＿。

　　B: ええ、そうですね。

2. A: この　テレビは　きむらさんの　テレビです＿＿＿。

　　B: いいえ。　たなかさんの　テレビです＿＿＿。

3. A: つくえの　うえに　ねこが　いますか。

　　B: いいえ。　つくえの　したに　います＿＿＿。

4. A: この　ドアは　おてあらいですか。

　　B: はい、そうです＿＿＿。

5. A: この　がっこうは　とても　ふるいです＿＿＿。

　　B: ええ、とても　ふるいです＿＿＿。

Name _____ Class _____ Date _____

そうごうれんしゅう　(Integration)

First draw a living room, keeping it simple. Then imagine that you are showing the living room to your new roommate. Write a short dialogue, using the following questions as cues.

Questions

1. どんな　へやですか。
2. へやに　まどが　ありますか。
3. どんな　まどが　ありますか。
4. まどの　ちかくに　なにが　ありますか。
5. へやの　みぎがわに　どんな　ものが　ありますか。
6. へやの　ひだりがわに　どんな　ものが　ありますか。
7. ドアの　ちかくに　なにが　ありますか。

A: _____

B: _____

A: _____

B: _____

A: _____

B: _____

A: _____

B: _____

≣ カタカナ (Katakana)
かたかな

Katakana ア～ソ
あ　そ

A. Write each **katakana**, following the correct stroke order. The arrows indicate the direction of each stroke.

ア	ア	﹃	ア					
イ	イ	ノ	イ					
ウ	ウ	｡	ｨ	ウ				
エ	エ	﹁	下	エ				
オ	オ	﹁	才	オ				
カ	カ	﹃	カ					
キ	キ	﹁	キ	キ				
ク	ク	﹀	ク					
ケ	ケ	﹀	﹂	ケ				
コ	コ	﹃	コ					
サ	サ	﹁	サ	サ				
シ	シ	﹀	﹁	シ				
ス	ス	﹃	ス					
セ	セ	﹃	セ					
ソ	ソ	﹀	ソ					

B. Practice writing each **katakana** ten times, following the correct stroke order.

ア										
イ										
ウ										
エ										
オ										
カ										
キ										
ク										
ケ										
コ										
サ										
シ										
ス										
セ										
ソ										

C. Practice writing each of the following words five times in **katakana.** Then guess its English meaning.

■ スイス   <u>スイス スイス スイス スイス スイス</u>   <u>Switzerland</u>

1. ケーキ   _____   _____

2. スキー   _____   _____

3. アイス   _____   _____

4. シーソー   _____   _____

5. キス   _____   _____

6. オアシス   _____   _____

Katakana タ〜ホ

A. Write each **katakana,** following the correct stroke order. The arrows indicate the direction of each stroke.

タ	タ	゛	ク	タ					
チ	チ	゛	ニ	チ					
ツ	ツ	゛	゛	ツ					
テ	テ	゛	二	テ					
ト	ト	‖	ド						
ナ	ナ	二	ナ						
ニ	ニ	゛	二						
ヌ	ヌ	フ	ヌ						

    Workbook: Chapter 3   35

ネ	ネ	゛	ヲ	ネ	ネ						
ノ	ノ	ノ									
ハ	ハ	ノ	バ								
ヒ	ヒ	ニ	匕								
フ	フ	ヲ									
ヘ	ヘ	ヘ									
ホ	ホ	二	サ	オ	ホ						

B. Practice writing each **katakana** ten times, following the correct stroke order.

タ											
チ											
ツ											
テ											
ト											
ナ											
ニ											
ヌ											
ネ											
ノ											

ハ										
ヒ										
フ										
ヘ										
ホ										

C. Practice writing each of the following words five times. Then write its English meaning.

■ カット   カット カット カット カット カット   cut

1. テスト   _____   _____

2. タッチ   _____   _____

3. カヌー   _____   _____

4. ネット   _____   _____

5. ノート   _____   _____

6. ハット   _____   _____

7. ヒーター   _____   _____

カタカナ　マ〜ン

A. Write each **katakana**, following the correct stroke order. The arrows indicate the direction of each stroke.

マ	マ	フ	マ						
ミ	ミ	ミ	ミ	ミ					
ム	ム	ム	ム						
メ	メ	ノ	メ						
モ	モ	ニ	ニ	モ					
ヤ	ヤ	フ	ヤ						
ユ	ユ	フ	ユ						
ヨ	ヨ	ヲ	ヲ	ヨ					
ラ	ラ	ニ	ラ						
リ	リ	リ	リ						
ル	ル	ノ	ル						
レ	レ	レ							
ロ	ロ	丨	フ	ロ					
ワ	ワ	ヽ	ワ						
ン	ン	ヽ	ン						

B. Practice writing each **katakana** ten times, following the correct stroke order.

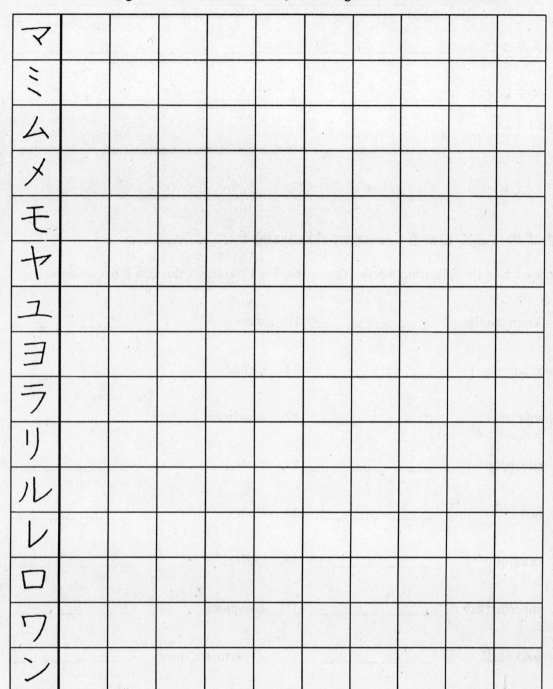

C. Practice writing each of the following words five times. Then write its English meaning.

1. アメリカ _____ _____

2. オーストラリア _____ _____

3. フランス   _____   _____

4. メキシコ   _____   _____

5. ステレオ   _____   _____

6. ノート   _____   _____

7. レストラン   _____   _____

カタカナの　ふくしゅう　(Summary of Katakana)

A. Write each of the following words. They appear in Chapters 1 through 5 of *Nakama 1*.

1. Asian studies	_____	10. shower	_____
2. Spain	_____	11. Canada	_____
3. sofa	_____	12. apartment	_____
4. television	_____	13. table	_____
5. bed	_____	14. door	_____
6. campus	_____	15. coffee	_____
7. supermarket	_____	16. computer	_____
8. backpack	_____	17. department store	_____
9. laboratory	_____	18. ballpoint pen	_____

B. Read each of the following words and write it in English.

■ コーラ   _cola_

1. マクドナルド _____   5. パイ   _____

2. フォーク   _____   6. ナイフ   _____

3. ガレージ   _____   7. オフィス   _____

4. エンジニア   _____   8. ガラス   _____

C. Read each of the following names of cities and write it in English.

1. ホンコン   _____   5. シドニー   _____

2. パリ   _____   6. モスクワ   _____

3. ニューヨーク _____   7. ボゴタ   _____

4. ホノルル   _____   8. カイロ   _____

D. Write your full name, the name of your home state or country, and your hometown in both **katakana** and English.

Name   _____

Home state or country   _____

Hometown   _____

だいよんか (Chapter 4)
にほんの　まちと　だいがく
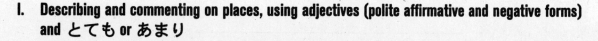 (Japanese Towns and Universities)

I. **Describing and commenting on places, using adjectives (polite affirmative and negative forms) and とても or あまり**

A. Write your answer to each of the following questions, using the appropriate form of each adjective.

■　～さんの　だいがくは　おおきいですか。
　　<u>ええ、とても　おおきいです。</u>

1. ～さんの　だいがくは　ふるいですか。

　　_____

2. としょかんは　りっぱですか。

　　_____

3. にほんごの　きょうしつは　ひろいですか。

　　_____

4. がくせいかいかんは　きれいですか。

　　_____

5. だいがくの　りょうは　いいですか。

　　_____

6. たいいくかんは　あかるいですか。

　　_____

7. しょくどうは　あたらしいですか。

　　_____

B. Complete the following conversations, using the appropriate form of the adjective.

■ A: さとうさん、さとうさんの　だいがくは　おおきいですか。
　　B: ええ、とても　<u>おおきいですよ</u>。

1. A: かとうさんの　いぬは　しずかですか。

　　B: いいえ、＿＿＿＿＿＿＿＿＿＿＿＿＿＿＿＿＿＿＿＿。

2. A: その　きっさてんは　あまり　＿＿＿＿＿＿＿＿＿＿＿＿＿＿＿＿＿よ。

　　あの　きっさてんは　どうですか？

　　B: そうですね。　あそこは　とても　きれいですよ。

3. A: その　たんすは　とても　＿＿＿＿＿＿＿＿＿＿＿＿＿＿＿＿＿ね。

　　B: ええ、わたしの　おばあさん (grandmother) の　たんすですよ。

4. A: やまださんの　かばんは　くろいですか。

　　B: いいえ、＿＿＿＿＿＿＿＿＿＿＿＿＿＿＿＿＿。

5. A: スミスさんの　うちは　すてきですね。
　　　　すみす

　　B: ええ、とても　＿＿＿＿＿＿＿＿＿＿＿＿＿＿＿＿＿ね。

II. Referring to things mentioned immediately before, using noun/adjective + の

A. Look at the following chart and write appropriate statements, using the information about the different schools in a university. Use adjective + の.

けいざいがくぶ	ほうがくぶ	こうがくぶ	きょうようがくぶ
おおきい ふるい りっぱ ゆうめい	ちいさい あたらしい しずか ゆうめい	あたらしい きれい りっぱ	ふるい おおきい きれい

■ おおきい　　おおきいのは　けいざいがくぶと　きょうようがくぶです。

1. ちいさい　　_____

2. きれい　　_____

3. あたらしい　　_____

4. りっぱ　　_____

5. ゆうめい　　_____

B. Fill in the blanks with appropriate expressions, using noun/adjective + の.

	やまだ	スミス	キム	リン
じしょ	りっぱ	きれい	あたらしい	ちいさい
ノート	あかい	しろい	あおい	くろい
きょうかしょ	きれい	ふるい	あたらしい	あたらしい

■ くろい　ノートは＿＿リンさんの＿＿ です。

1. ちいさい　じしょは＿＿＿＿＿＿＿＿＿＿＿＿＿＿＿＿ です。

＿＿＿＿＿＿＿＿＿＿＿＿＿＿＿＿ は　スミスさんのです。

2. しろい　ノートは＿＿＿＿＿＿＿＿＿＿＿＿＿＿ です。あかいのは

＿＿＿＿＿＿＿＿＿＿＿＿＿ です。

3. きれいな　きょうかしょは＿＿＿＿＿＿＿＿＿＿＿＿＿＿ です。

ふるいのは ＿＿＿＿＿＿＿＿＿＿＿＿＿ です。

4. やまださんの　ノートは　あかいです。でも、＿＿＿＿＿＿＿＿＿＿ は

あおいです。

5. キムさんの　きょうかしょは　あたらしいです。＿＿＿＿＿＿＿＿＿

も　あたらしいです。

III. Referring to things, using これ, それ, あれ, どれ

A. Look at the following map. Yamada-san is showing her college campus to Kim-san. They are now standing right in front of the student union (A and B). Complete their conversation, using これ, それ, あれ. The — marks on the map indicate the front entrance of each building.

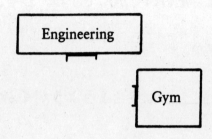

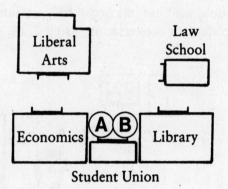

Student Union

キム: _____これ_____ は　がくせいかいかんですか。

やまだ: ええ、そうです。

キム: _____ は　ほうがくぶですか。

やまだ: いいえ、そうじゃありません。　あれは　こうがくぶの

たてものですよ。

<ruby>キ<rt>き</rt>ム<rt>む</rt></ruby>: そうですか。 おおきい たてものですね。

やまだ: ええ。 それから、＿＿＿＿＿＿＿＿ は たいいくかんですよ。

<ruby>キ<rt>き</rt>ム<rt>む</rt></ruby>: りっぱな たいいくかんですね。じゃあ、＿＿＿＿＿＿＿＿ は

なんですか。

やまだ: ＿＿＿＿＿＿＿＿ は きょうようがくぶですよ。

<ruby>キ<rt>き</rt>ム<rt>む</rt></ruby>: そうですか。

B. Tanaka-san is helping Smith-san, who has just begun to learn Japanese. Look at the following illustration and complete their conversation, using これ, それ, あれ, and どれ.

スミス: あのう、すみません。 ＿これ＿ は にほんごで なんと

いいますか。

たなか: えんぴつと いいます。

スミス：　そうですか。　じゃあ、_____ は　なんと　いいますか。

たなか：　これですか。　これは　けしゴムと　いいます。

スミス：　そうですか。じゃあ、_____ は　なんと　いいますか。

たなか：　_____ は　いすです。

スミス：　_____ は　なんと　いいますか。

たなか：　ドアと　いいます。

スミス：　そうですか。　えいごですね。_____ は　notebook と

　　　　　いいますか。

たなか：　いいえ、_____ は　ノートと　いいます。

　　　　　　　　　　　　　　　　　　　　　　　Workbook: Chapter 4　　**49**

IV. Using は and が

Fill in the blanks in each of the following conversations with は or が.

1. A: あのう、すみません。 ゆうびんきょく＿＿＿＿ どこに ありますか。

   B: ゆうびんきょくですか。 そこですよ。

   A: そうですか。 どうも、ありがとう ございます。

2. A: リー^りさん＿＿＿＿ どの ひとですか。

   B: あの ひとです。

3. A: どれ＿＿＿＿ やまださんの けしゴム^{ごむ}ですか。

   B: これです。

4. A: どの たてもの＿＿＿＿ えきですか。

   B: あれです。

   A: おおきいですね。 じゃあ、 こうばん＿＿＿＿ どれですか。

   B: そこに ちいさい たてもの＿＿＿＿ ありますね。 それですよ。

5. A: そこに いぬ＿＿＿＿ いますよ。

   B: えっ。どこですか。

   A: そこに あかい かばん＿＿＿＿ ありますね。 いぬ＿＿＿＿

      その かばんの うしろに います。

V. Expressing location, using ～は　～に　あります／います and ～は　です

A. Look at the following illustration. A police officer is standing in front of the police box. People come up to the police officer to ask about different places in the neighborhood. Write his answers, using ここ, そこ, or あそこ.

■ A: こうばんは　どこに　ありますか。

　B: <u>ここです。／ここに　あります。</u>

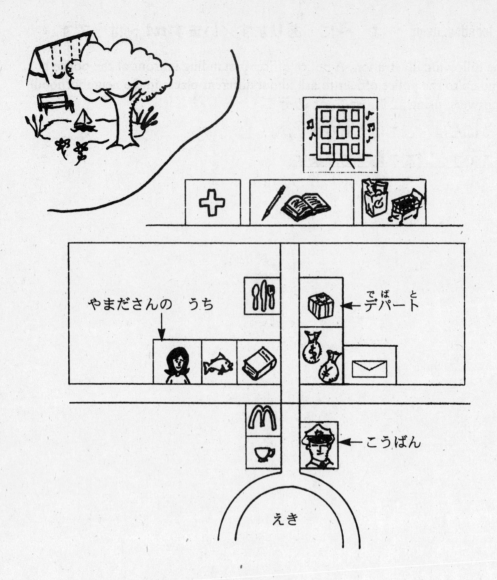

やまださんの　うち

でぱーと
デパート

こうばん

えき

1. こうえんは　どこに　ありますか。

_____

2. ほんやは　どこに　ありますか。

_____

3. きっさてんは　どこに　ありますか。

_____

4. デパートは　どこに　ありますか。
   _{でば}_と

_____

5　がっこうは　どこに　ありますか。

_____

B. Write your answer to each of the following questions, using 〜に　あります. Note that ごりょうしん means *your parents*.

■　じょうとうだいがくは　どこに　ありますか。

　　<u>とうきょうに　あります。</u>

1.　ごりょうしんの　うちは　どこに　ありますか。

_____

2.　ごりょうしんは　どこに　いますか。

_____

3.　うちは　どこに　ありますか。

_____

4.　だいがくの　ほんやは　どこに　ありますか。

_____

5.　にほんごの　せんせいは　どこに　いますか。

_____

Name _____ Class _____ Date _____

そうごうれんしゅう (Integration)

A. Look at the following map. Michiko-san and Alice-san are in front of the student union, and Michiko-san is pointing at different buildings. Complete the following conversation, using the appropriate こそあど words.

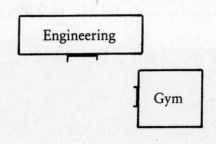

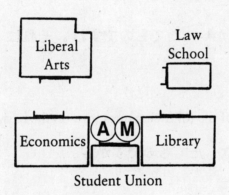

Student Union

みちこ： アリスさん、__そこ__ に しろい たてものが ありますね。

アリス： ええ。

みちこ： _____ (1) は きょうようがくぶです。

アリス： おおきい たてものですね。じゃあ、_____ (2) たてものは

なんですか。

みちこ： _____ (3) ですか。 としょかんですよ。

アリス： りっぱな たてものですね。 じゃあ、としょかんの まえの

たてものは なんですか。

みちこ：　　　え、＿＿＿＿＿ (4) ですか。

アリス：　　　＿＿＿＿＿ (5) に　ちいさい　たてものが　ありますね。

みちこ：　　　ああ、＿＿＿＿＿ (6) は　ほうがくぶの　たてものですよ。

アリス：　　　そうですか。じゃ、こうがくぶは　＿＿＿＿＿ (7) に

　　　　　　　ありますか。

みちこ：　　　＿＿＿＿＿ (8) です。

アリス：　　　とても　たかい　たてものですね。それに　とても　きれい

　　　　　　　ですね。

B. Write your answer to each of the following questions on the basis of the conversation in A.

1. としょかんは　どんな　たてものですか。

＿＿＿＿＿＿＿＿＿＿＿＿＿＿＿＿＿＿＿＿＿＿＿＿＿＿＿＿

2. こうがくぶは　どんな　たてものですか。

＿＿＿＿＿＿＿＿＿＿＿＿＿＿＿＿＿＿＿＿＿＿＿＿＿＿＿＿

3. どの　たてものが　ちいさいですか。

＿＿＿＿＿＿＿＿＿＿＿＿＿＿＿＿＿＿＿＿＿＿＿＿＿＿＿＿

4. きょうようがくぶは　どんな　たてものですか。

＿＿＿＿＿＿＿＿＿＿＿＿＿＿＿＿＿＿＿＿＿＿＿＿＿＿＿＿

だいごか　(Chapter 5)
まいにちの　せいかつ　1
(Daily Routine 1)

I. Telling time, using numbers, counters, and the particle に

A. Write the following time expressions in **hiragana**.

1. 9:50 A.M.　　　　　　_____

2. 11:15 P.M.　　　　　_____

3. 12:03　　　　　　　_____

4. 10:30　　　　　　　_____

5. 4 hours, 14 minutes　_____

6. 6 hours　　　　　　_____

B. Write your answer to each of the following questions.

1. いま　なんじですか。

_____

2. まいにち　なんじに　おきますか。

_____

3. まいばん　なんじに　ねますか。

_____

4. にほんごの　じゅぎょうは　なんじに　はじまりますか。

_____

5. にほんごの　じゅぎょうは　なんじに　おわりますか。

_____

6. にほんごの　じゅぎょうは　なんようびに　ありますか。

_____

II. Expressing what one does and where one does it, using the particles に, で, and を

A. Complete each of the following sentences by filling in the blanks with the correct particle (を or に) and the correct verb from the box.

いきます　よみます　たべます　します　みます　かえります

■ あさごはん <u> を </u>　<u> たべます </u>。

1. ほん ____ _____。

2. うち ____ _____。

3. だいがく ____ _____。

4. テレビ ____ _____。

5. しゅくだい ____ _____。

6. ひるごはん ____ _____。

B. Complete each of the following sentences by filling in the blanks with the correct particle. Particles included in this exercise are を for a direct object, に for a destination, goal, or point in time, and で for the location of an action.

■ くじ <u> に </u>　はじまります。

1. しちじ ____ おきます。

2. シャワー ____ あびます。

3. うち ____ ねます。

4. おふろ＿＿＿＿ はえります。

5. ろくじ＿＿＿＿ ばんごはん＿＿＿＿ たべます。

6. ごじはん＿＿＿＿ アパート＿＿＿＿ かえります。
   　　　　　　　　あ　ば　と

III. Expressing routines, future actions, or events, using the polite present forms of verbs

Complete the following chart by writing the ～ません form of each verb in the second column. Then write the English meaning of the verb in the third column.

～ます	～ません	English
かえります	かえりません	to return; to go home
1. たべます		
2. きます		
3. はじまります		
4. ねます		
5. よみます		
6. みます		
7. はいります		
8. おきます		
9. します		

IV. Expressing frequency of actions, using adverbs

A. Complete each of the following sentences by filling in the blanks with the correct particle and a verb from the box. Change the verb to the negative if necessary. In some sentences, the first **hiragana** is given to help you.

> します　あびます　いきます　たべます　きます　よみます　かえります
> おきます　みます　ねます

■ よく　テレビ ＿を＿　＿みます＿。

1. ほん＿＿　よく　＿＿＿＿＿＿＿＿。

2. やまださんは　ぜんぜん　じゅぎょう＿＿　き＿＿＿＿＿＿＿＿。

3. ときどき　レストラン＿＿　ばんごはん＿＿　＿＿＿＿＿＿＿＿。

4. たいてい　あさ　ろくじ＿＿　＿＿＿＿＿＿＿＿。

5. えいが＿＿　あまり　み＿＿＿＿＿＿。

6. たいてい　ごじ＿＿　うち＿＿　か＿＿＿＿＿＿。

7. すずきさんは　まいあさ　いつも　シャワー＿＿　＿＿＿＿＿＿＿＿。

8. さとうさんは　いつも　ごご　じゅういちじ＿＿　＿＿＿＿＿＿＿。

9. スミスさんは　とても　よく　べんきょう＿＿　＿＿＿＿＿＿＿＿。

B. Write your answer to each of the following questions, using a frequency word.

■ としょかんに　よく　いきますか。
　はい、ときどき　いきます。　or　いいえ、あまり　いきません。

1. あさ　シャワーを　あびますか。

_____

2. いつも　あさごはんを　たべますか。

_____

3. よく　にほんごの　ほんを　よみますか。

_____

4. よく　としょかんで　べんきょうしますか。

_____

5. よく　おふろに　はいりますか

_____

6. よく　えいがを　みますか。

_____

7. いつも　なんじに　ねますか。

_____

V. Expressing approximate time and duration, using ごろ or ぐらい

Write your answer to each of the following questions about yourself. Use ごろ or ぐらい.

■ まいにち　ほんを　なんじかん　よみますか。
　　まいにち　にじかんぐらい　よみます。

1. まいあさ　なんじに　おきますか。

   _____

2. まいばん　なんじに　ねますか。

   _____

3. まいにち　テレビを　なんじかん　みますか。

   _____

4. こんばん　なんじかん　べんきょうしますか。

   _____

5. きょう　いつ　うちに　かえりますか。

   _____

6. あした　なんじかん　じゅぎょうが　ありますか。

   _____

7. げつようびに　なんじに　だいがくに　いきますか。

   _____

そうごうれんしゅう (Integration)

First read the following passage describing a typical week in a teacher's life. Then write your answer to each of the questions that follow.

山本先生は私の日本語の先生です。先生は毎朝七時ごろ起きます。たいてい朝ごはんを食べます。そして、いつも八時ごろ大学に行きます。先生は日本語の授業が毎日二時間あります。よく学生会館で昼ごはんを食べます。毎日五時にうちに帰ります。夜はたいていレストランで晩ごはんを食べます。テレビはぜんぜん見ません。土曜日にときどきデパートに行きます。そして、先生は映画をよく見ます。

1. やまもとせんせいは　なんじに　おきますか。

　　_____

2. せんせいは　あさ　なにを　しますか。

　　_____

3. せんせいは　いつ　だいがくに　きますか。

　　_____

4. せんせいは　なんじかんぐらい　にほんごの　じゅぎょうが　ありますか。

_____

5. せんせいは　なんじごろ　うちに　かえりますか。

_____

6. せんせいは　ばんごはんを　どこで　たべますか。

_____

7. せんせいは　テレビを　よく　みますか。

_____

8. せんせいは　どようびに　なにを　しますか。

_____

だいろっか　(Chapter 6)
まいにちの　せいかつ　2
(Daily Routine 2)

I. Expressing a means, using で; expressing starting and ending points, using から～まで; expressing *to whom*, using に; expressing *together with*, using と

A. Complete each of the following sentences by filling in the blanks with the correct particle.

1. ともだち _____　うち _____　ばんごはん _____　たべます。

2. げつようび _____　りょうしん _____　でんわ _____　かけました。

3. はちじ _____　くじ _____　にほんご _____　じゅぎょう _____

    あります。

4. としょかん _____　ともだち _____　てがみ _____　かきました。

5. うち _____　だいがく _____　じてんしゃ _____　いきます。

B. Write your answer to each of the following questions about yourself.

1. だれに　よく　てがみを　かきますか。

    _____

2. だれに　よく　でんわを　かけますか。

    _____

3. だれと　べんきょうしますか。

    _____

4. なんで　だいがくに　きますか。

    _____

5. にほんごの　じゅぎょうは　なんじから　なんじまで　ありますか。

_____

II. Talking about past events, using polite past verbs and polite past adjectives

A. Complete each of the following charts.

	Past tense affirmative	Past tense negative
はちじ（に）おきます	おきました	おきませんでした
1. ほん（　）かいます		
2. ともだち（　）でんわ（　）かけます		
3. ごはん（　）つくります		
4. ざっし（　）よみます		
5. ビデオ（　）みます		
6. うち（　　）だいがく（　　）あるいて いきます		
7. ともだち（　）はなします		
8. おんがく（　）ききます		
9. ともだち（　）てがみ（　）かきます		
10. でかけます		

	Polite Past Tense Affirmative	Polite Past Tense Negative
おおきい	おおきかったです	おおきくありませんでした おおきくなかったです
11. たいへん		
12. いい		
13. しずか		
14. たのしい		
15. むずかしい		
16. ひま		
17. おもしろい		
18. きれい		

B. Complete each of the following sentences by filling in the blanks with the correct form of the verb and adjective.

■ A: きのう　しんぶんを　<u>　よみました　</u>か。
　　　　　　　　　　　　　　よみます

B: いいえ、<u>　よみませんでした　</u>。

1. A: きのうの　しけんは＿＿＿＿＿＿＿＿＿＿＿＿＿＿か。
　　　　　　　　　　　　　　むずかしい

　　　B: いいえ、あまり _____。

2. A: きのう　しゅくだいを _____か。
　　　　　　　　　　　　　　　　　　　　します

　　　B: ええ、 _____。

3. A: きのうは _____か。
　　　　　　　　　　　　いそがしい

　　　B: ええ、とても _____。

4. A: きのう　てがみを _____か。
　　　　　　　　　　　　　　　　かきます

　　　B: いいえ、 _____。　でも、せんしゅう

　　　_____。

5. A: きのうは _____か。
　　　　　　　　　　　　たいへん

　　　B: いいえ、　あまり _____。

　　　　　　　　　　　Workbook: Chapter 6　　75

III. Expressing frequency and quantity, using counter expressions

A. Fill in the blanks with the appropriate expressions of frequency, extent, or duration, using the following schedule.

■ けいざいがくの　じゅぎょうは　＿いっしゅうかんに　にど＿　あります。

日 (にち)	月 (げつ)	火 (か)	水 (すい)	木 (もく)	金 (きん)	土 (ど)
30 テレビ(3) レストラン ともだちにてがみをかきます	**1** にほんご(1) べんきょう(2) アルバイト(2)	**2** にほんご(1) けいざいがく(1.5) アルバイト(2) ばんごはんをつくります ほんをよみます(1)	**3** にほんご(1) べんきょう(2) ほんをよみます(1) ともだちにでんわをかけます	**4** にほんご(1) けいざいがく(1.5) アルバイト(2) ばんごはんをつくります テレビ(2)	**5** にほんご(1) うんどう(1) べんきょう(2) アルバイト(2) テレビ(2) ともだちにでんわをかけます	**6** そうじをします せんたくをします えいがをみます ばんごはんをつくります
7 デパート ばんごはんをつくります	**8** にほんご(1) べんきょう(2) アルバイト(2) ほんをよみます(1) ともだちにでんわをかけます	**9** にほんご(1) けいざいがく(1.5) アルバイト(2) ばんごはんをつくります	**10** にほんご(1) べんきょう(2) テレビ(2)	**11** にほんご(1) けいざいがく(1.5) アルバイト(2) ばんごはんをつくります ほんをよみます(1) ともだちにでんわをかけます	**12** にほんご(1) うんどう(1) べんきょう(2) アルバイト(2) テレビ(2)	**13** そうじをします せんたくをします レストラン りょうしんにでんわをかけます

1. にほんごの　じゅぎょうは ＿＿＿＿＿＿＿＿＿＿＿＿＿＿＿＿ あります。

2. へやを ＿＿＿＿＿＿＿＿＿＿＿＿＿ そうじします。

3. アルバイトを ＿＿＿＿＿＿＿＿＿＿じかん　します。

4. ばんごはんを ＿＿＿＿＿＿＿＿＿＿＿＿＿ つくります。

5. レストランに ＿＿＿＿＿＿＿＿＿＿＿＿＿ いきます。

6. りょうしんに ＿＿＿＿＿＿＿＿＿＿＿＿＿ でんわを　かけます。

7. ともだちに ＿＿＿＿＿＿＿＿＿＿＿＿＿ でんわを　かけます。

B. Answer the following questions using 〜に 〜ぐらい.

■ いちにちに　なんじかんぐらい　べんきょうしますか。

　いちにちに　さんじかんぐらい　べんきょうします。

　よく　うんどうを　しますか。

　いいえ、あまり　しません。　いっかげつに　いちどぐらい　します。

1. いっしゅうかんに　なんじかん　アルバイトを　しますか。

＿＿＿＿＿＿＿＿＿＿＿＿＿＿＿＿＿＿＿＿＿＿＿＿＿＿＿＿＿＿

2. いちにちに　どのぐらい　テレビを　みますか。

＿＿＿＿＿＿＿＿＿＿＿＿＿＿＿＿＿＿＿＿＿＿＿＿＿＿＿＿＿＿

3. いっしゅうかんに　なんかいぐらい　としょかんに　いきますか。

＿＿＿＿＿＿＿＿＿＿＿＿＿＿＿＿＿＿＿＿＿＿＿＿＿＿＿＿＿＿

4. よく　びょういんに　いきますか。

＿＿＿＿＿＿＿＿＿＿＿＿＿＿＿＿＿＿＿＿＿＿＿＿＿＿＿＿＿＿

5. よく　ごはんを　つくりますか。

＿＿＿＿＿＿＿＿＿＿＿＿＿＿＿＿＿＿＿＿＿＿＿＿＿＿＿＿＿＿

6. よく　てがみを　かきますか。

_____

IV. Using double particles with the topic marker は, the contrast marker は, and the similarity marker も

A. Complete each of the following sentences by filling in the blanks with the correct particle(s) for a topic.

■ きのう　ほんやに　いきました。その　ほんや <u>には</u>　にほんごの　じしょが
ありました。

1. きのう　ほんやに　いきました。その　ほんや_____　にほんごの

   じしょを　かいました。

2. きのう　しけんが　ありました。その　しけん_____　とても

   むずかしかったです。

3. きのう　スミス(すみす)さんに　てがみを　かきました。　スミス(すみす)さん_____

   よく　でんわで　はなします。

4. くじですね。くじ_____　おもしろい　テレビ(てれび)が　あります。

5. きのう　きっさてんで　ばんごはんを　たべました。その

   きっさてん_____　とても　ふるかったです。

B. Complete each of the following conversations by filling in the blanks with the correct particle(s) and verb.

■ A: ニュー(にゅ)ヨー(よ)ク(く)は　おおきいですね。

　B: ええ。

　A: パリ(ばり)(Paris)_<u>も</u>_　おおきいですか。

　B: いいえ、パリ(ばり)_<u>は</u>_　あまり　<u>おおきくありません。</u>

1. A: だいがくに　なんで　きますか。

   B: たいてい　じてんしゃで　きます。

   A: バス_____　_____か。

   B: いいえ、バス_____　_____。

2. A: ディズニーランド (Disneyland) は　アメリカに　ありますね。

   B: ええ、とうきょう_____　_____よ。

   A: ああ、そうですか。

3. A: すずきさんは　じゅぎょうが　ありますか。

   B: はい、１０じはんに　あります。

   A: １１じ３０ぷん_____　_____か。

   B: ええ、１１じはん_____　_____。

4. A: きのうは　いそがしかったですね。

   B: ええ。　でも　きょう_____　あまり

   _____ね。

   A: そうですね。

V. Expressing a reason, using ～から, and expressing *but*, using が

A. Write a statement that combines the two sentences, using either ～から or が, whichever is appropriate. You must decide which of the two sentences should come first.

■ きょうは　べんきょうします。　あした　しけんが　あります。

　あした　しけんが　ありますから、きょうは　べんきょうします。

1. わたしは　はちじに　おきます。　ジョーンズさんは　ろくじに　おきます。

_____

2. ごはんを　つくりました。　ともだちが　うちに　きました。

_____

3. こんばん　えいがを　みます。あした　しけんが　あります。

_____

4. きのう　いそがしかったです。　アルバイトを　しました。

_____

5. しゅくだいが　まいにち　あります。　たいへんです。

_____

6. このほんは　むずかしかったです。　とても　おもしろかったです。

_____

B. Write your answer to each of the following questions, using ～から.

■ どの　スーパーに　よく　いきますか。　どうしてですか。

　わたしの　うちの　ちかくに　ありますから、　ペイレス (Pay Less)
に　よく　いきます。

1. どの　スーパーに　よく　いきますか。

_____

2. どこで　よく　ひるごはんを　たべますか。

_____

3. どの　きっさてんに　よく　いきますか。

_____

4. どの　しんぶんを　よく　かいますか。

_____

5. だれと　でんわで　よく　はなしますか。

_____

そうごうれんしゅう (Integration)

A. Write your answer to each of the following questions about what you did or didn't do last week. If you don't know a Japanese word, you should ask your instructor about it.

1. せんしゅうは　どうでしたか。

_____

2. まいにち　なんじごろ　おきましたか。

_____

3. げつようびから　きんようびまで　どんな　じゅぎょうが　ありましたか。

_____

4. にほんごの　じゅぎょうで　なにを　しましたか。

_____

5. じゅぎょうで　なにが　むずかしかったですか／やさしかったですか。
   どうして　むずかしかったですか／やさしかったですか。

_____

_____

6. ごご　なにを　しましたか。　いっしゅうかんに／いちにちに　どのくらい
　　しましたか。

_____

_____

7. しゅうまつには　なにを　しましたか。どうでしたか。

_____

_____

B. Write a composition, using your answers in exercise A.

■　せんしゅうは　とても　いそがしかったです。　げつようびからきんようび
　　まで　まいにち　じゅぎょうが　さんじかん　ありました。にほんごの
　　じゅぎょうは　まいにち　あさ　じゅうじに　あります。せんしゅうの
　　きんようびには　にほんごの　テスト（てすと）が　ありましたから、まいばん
　　べんきょうしました。　いちにちに　にじかんぐらい　べんきょう
　　しましたが、しけんは　むずかしかったです。せんしゅうは　しけんが
　　ありましたから、あまり　うんどうを　しませんでした。でも、どようびと
　　にちようびには　うんどうを　さんじかんぐらい　しました。　とても
　　たのしかったです。

_____

_____

_____

_____

_____

_____

_____

_____

_____

_____

だいななか
すきな ことと すきな もの
(Activities and Hobbies)

I. Expressing likes and dislikes, using すき or きらい

A. Write the appropriate particle or word in each of the following blanks, using the information in the chart. A smiling face indicates something the person likes (すきです). A neutral face indicates the person's indifference (あまり　すきじゃありません). A frowning face indicates the person's dislike (すきじゃありません).

山田(やまだ)　　ジョンソン　　ブラウン

バナナ

トマト

にんじん

りんご

1. 山田(やまだ)さんは _____ と _____ ____ すきです。

　　でも、_____ は　あまり _____ ありません。

2. ブラウンさんは　バナナー _____ ____ _____ 。

　　でも、りんごは _____ 。

3. ジョンソンさんは _____ や _____ ____

　　すきです。でも、_____ 。

4. 山田さんの ＿＿＿＿＿＿＿＿＿＿＿＿＿＿ たべものは　バナナです。

ブラウンさん ＿＿＿ バナナ ＿＿＿ ＿＿＿＿＿＿。

5. ＿＿＿＿＿＿＿ は　トマトや　りんごが　すきです。

6. ＿＿＿＿＿＿＿ は　にんじんが　あまり ＿＿＿＿＿＿＿＿＿＿＿。

B. Write your answer to each of the following questions, using でも and は to indicate a contrast.

■ どんな　スポーツが　すきですか。どんな　スポーツが　きらいですか。
ぼくは　やきゅうが　すきです。でも、フットボールは　あまり　すきじゃ
ありません。

1. どんな　スポーツが　すきですか。どんな　スポーツが　きらいですか。

＿＿＿＿＿＿＿＿＿＿＿＿＿＿＿＿＿＿＿＿＿＿＿＿＿＿＿＿

2. どんな　たべものが　すきですか。どんな　たべものが　きらいですか。

＿＿＿＿＿＿＿＿＿＿＿＿＿＿＿＿＿＿＿＿＿＿＿＿＿＿＿＿

3. どんな　おんがくが　すきですか。どんな　おんがくが　きらいですか。

＿＿＿＿＿＿＿＿＿＿＿＿＿＿＿＿＿＿＿＿＿＿＿＿＿＿＿＿

4. どんな　アパート／うちが　すきですか。どんな　アパート／うちが　きら
いですか。

＿＿＿＿＿＿＿＿＿＿＿＿＿＿＿＿＿＿＿＿＿＿＿＿＿＿＿＿

II. Making noun phrases, using の and the plain present affirmative form of the verb (dictionary form)

A. Complete the following chart. First identify whether the verb is irregular, a る-verb, or an う-verb. Then change the verb from the ～ます form to the dictionary form.

Verbs in ます	Verb Type	Dictionary Form
よみます	う	よむ
1. うたいます		
2. たべます		
3. ききます		
4. おきます		
5. ねます		
6. とります		
7. います		
8. します		
9. のみます		
10. およぎます		
11. かえります		
12. きます		
13. あそびます		

B. Rewrite each sentence using の to turn the verb form into a noun phrase.

■ 私（わたし）は テレビを よく みます。

　　私（わたし）は テレビを みるのが すきです。

1. 大川（おおかわ）さんは 山（やま）の しゃしんを よく とります。

　　_____

2. ジョンソンさんは テニスを よく します。

　　_____

3. ホワイトさんは　クラシックを　よく　ききます。

_____

4. グリーンさんは　ファミコンで　よく　あそびます。

_____

5. きむらさんは　よく　川に　いきます。

_____

C. Look at the following chart and describe each person's preferences. Use でも and は for contrast.

■　山田さんは　コーヒーを　のむのが　すきです。
　　でも、ビールを　のむのは　すきじゃありません。

	😊	☹️
山田	コーヒーを　のみます	ビールを　のみます
1. 田中	しずかな　おんがくを　ききます	パーティを　します
2. 大川	ふるい　えいがを　みます	あたらしい　えいがを　みます
3. 上田	山に　いきます	川に　いきます
4. 川上	ハイキングを　します	ジョギングを　します
5. 中山	しんぶんを　よみます	きょうかしょを　よみます

1. _____

_____

2. _____

_____

3. _____

_____

4. _____

_____

5. _____

_____

III. Listing nouns, using や

Write your answer to each of the following questions, using や or と, whichever is appropriate.

■ なにを　よく　たべますか。
　　にくや　やさいを　たべます。

1. しゅうまつに　どこに　いきますか。

_____

2. 日本語の　じゅぎょうは　なんようびに　ありますか。

_____

3. どんな　えいがが　すきですか。

_____

4. どんな　ざっしが　すきですか。

_____

5. どこで　ひるごはんを　たべますか。

_____

6. 本屋は　どこに　ありますか。

_____

IV. Making comparisons, using いちばん and 〜の　ほうが　〜より

A. Write the correct question for each of the following answers. Use いちばん and the appropriate adjective.

　　ことばの　リスト：　せかい　world　しゅう　state

■ ミシシッピー川 (Mississippi River)

　　　アメリカで　いちばん　大きい川は　どの川ですか。

1. ハワイ

　　_____

2. ロシア

　　_____

3. エベレスト山 (Mt. Everest)

　　_____

4. アラスカ

　　_____

5. ハーバード大学 (Harvard University)

　　_____

B. Write your answer to each of the following questions, using いちばん.

■ どんな　スポーツを　いちばん　よくしますか。

　　　私は　テニスを　いちばん　よく　します。

1. どの　レストランに　いちばん　よく　いきますか。

　　_____

2. どんな　スポーツを　みるのが　いちばん　すきですか。

　　_____

3. きっさてんで　なにを　いちばん　よく　のみますか。

_____

4. アメリカの　たべものの　中^{なか}で　なにが　いちばん　おいしいですか。

_____

5. どの　クラスが　いちばん　すきですか。

_____

C. For each of the following sets of items, write a sentence comparing the two items, using the adjective in parentheses.

■　ロサンゼルス　サンフランシスコ　（大^{おお}きい）
　　ロサンゼルスの　ほうが　サンフランシスコより　大^{おお}きいです。

1. 中国^{ちゅうごく}　日本^{にほん}　（大^{おお}きい）

_____

2. ニューヨーク　ロンドン　（ふるい）

_____

3. 大学院生^{だいがくいんせい}　大学生^{だいがくせい}　（いそがしい）

_____

4. カタカナ　かんじ　（たいへん）

_____

5. 富士山^{ふじさん}　エベレスト山^{ざん}　（たかい）

_____

D. For each of the following sets of items, write a sentence comparing the two items, supplying an adjective of your own.

■ とうきょう　ニューヨーク

　とうきょうの　ほうが　ニューヨークより　すこし　大^{おお}きいです。

1. アメリカ　日本^{にほん}

_____

2. ドイツの　くるま　アメリカの　くるま

_____

3. 日本語^{にほんご}　スペイン語^ご

_____

4. クラシック　ロック

_____

V. Requesting and giving an explanation or a confirmation, using the prenominal forms of adjectives and the plain present forms of verbs +んです

A. Complete the following charts by supplying the prenominal form of each adjective and the plain present form of each verb.

Adjectives	Type	Affirmative + んです	Negative + んです
おお 大きい	い	おお 大きいんです	おお 大きくないんです
1. きれい	な		
2. たかい			
3. ひろい			
4. ゆうめい			
5. あかい			
6. りっぱ			

Verbs	Type	Affirmative + んです	Negative + んです
いきます	う	いくんです	いかないんです
1. およぎます			
2. します			
3. おきます			
4. あそびます			
5. よみます			
6. でかけます			
7. きます			
8. べんきょうします			
9. とります			
10. うたいます			

B. The following conversations are somewhat awkward because some sentences use ます／
ません instead of んです. Underline the parts that would need to be changed, and supply
the correct 〜んです-form.

■ A: どうして　にくを　<u>たべませんか。</u>

<u>たべないんですか</u>

B: にくは　<u>きらいです。</u>

<u>きらいなんです</u>

1. A: よく　バナナを　たべますね。

_____

B: ええ、バナナが　とても　すきです。

_____

2. (B is not playing computer games while others are participating.)

　A: ファミコンを　しませんか。

　_____

　B: ええ、あまり　すきじゃありません。

　_____

3. A: どうして　うちに　かえりますか。

　_____

　B: ともだちが　きます。

　_____

4. (At midnight, A sees roommate, B, leaving his/her apartment.)

　A: いま　でかけますか。

　_____

　B: ええ、あさごはんの　たまごが　ありません。

　_____

5. A: どうして　その　アパートは　きらいですか。

　_____

　B: 小さいです。

　_____

そうごうれんしゅう

A. Write your answer to each of the following questions about your best friend (わたしの　いちばん　いいともだち).

1. いちばん　いい　ともだちは　だれですか。

　_____

2. その 人は どんな たべものが すきですか。どんな たべものが きらいですか。

_____

3. その 人は 学生ですか。 いま どこに いますか。

_____

4. その 人は スポーツが すきですか。 よく しますか。

_____

5. その 人は しゅうまつに よく なにを しますか。

_____

B. Using your answers from exercise A as a guide, write a description of your best friend. Remember to use conjunctions such as でも, そして, and それから and particles such as は, も, と, and や to make smooth transitions between your ideas.

_____

_____

_____

_____

_____

_____

_____

_____

_____

かく　れんしゅう

A. Look at the charts on pages 228–230 of your textbook and write each **kanji** ten times following the correct stroke order.

山									
日									
田									
人									
上									
下									
中									
大									
小									
本									
学									
生									
先									
私									
川									

B. Rewrite each sentence using **kanji** you have learned. Numbers in parentheses indicate the number of **kanji** you should use.

1. やまださんは　よく　かわで　およぎます。(3)

   _____

2. わたしの　せんせいは　にほんじんです。(6)

   _____

3. つくえの　うえに　ねこが　います。つくえの　したにも　います。(2)

   _____

4. この　クラスの　がくせいの　なかで　どの　ひとが　いちばん　よく
   べんきょうしますか。(4)

   _____

5. かわかみさんと　やまもとさんの　なまえの　かんじは　よみ (reading) が
   むずかしいです。(4)

   _____

だい八か
かいもの　(Shopping)

I.　Making a request, using the て-form of a verb + 下^{くだ}さい

A. Complete the chart, following the example.

Verb	English	Verb type	て-form
くる	to come	irregular	きて
1. べんきょうする			
2. いく			
3. みせる			
4. かう			
5. おきる			
6. つつむ			
7. とる			
8. かく			
9. もつ			
10. だす			
11. およぐ			
12. いる			

B. Write three requests that you would address to a salesperson and three requests that you would address to your instructor.

■ Salesperson <u>その　とけいを　とって下さい。</u>

　Instructor　　<u>ゆっくり　はなして下さい。</u>

Salesperson

1. _____

2. _____

3. _____

Instructor

4. _____

5. _____

6. _____

II. Using Chinese origin numbers, 100 and above

A. Write the arabic numerals for the following numbers.

1. <ruby>四千五百六<rt>よんせんごひゃくろく</rt></ruby> _____

2. <ruby>百 八<rt>ひゃくはち</rt></ruby> _____

3. <ruby>一万七千<rt>いちまんななせん</rt></ruby> _____

4. <ruby>三百四十万<rt>さんびゃくよんじゅうまん</rt></ruby> _____

5. <ruby>八万三千五十五<rt>はちまんさんぜんごじゅうご</rt></ruby> _____

6. <ruby>二十九万六千百三十<rt>にじゅうきゅうまんろくせんひゃくさんじゅう</rt></ruby> _____

B. Write the pronunciation of the following numbers in **hiragana**.

1. 12,456 _____

2. 3,333,333 _____

3. 48,862 _____

4. 6,670 _____

5. 55,799 _____

III. Referring to quantities with numbers and counters, using まい, 本, ひき, さつ and Japanese origin numbers

A. Look at each of the numbered illustrations and write a sentence describing each item and quantity, following the example. Do not use **kanji**.

■ けしゴムが みっつ あります。

■

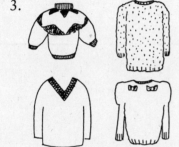

1.

2.

3.

4.

1. _____

2. _____

3. _____

4. _____

B. You need to go grocery shopping and have your list ready. Now write what you will say to the salesperson in Japanese.

■ 6 bananas <u>バナナを　ろっぽん　下さい。</u>

3 tomatoes	_____
5 fish	_____
10 bottles of beer	_____
2 apples	_____
7 carrots	_____

IV. Referring to prices and floor levels, using えん and かい

A. Look at the following price chart, which shows unit prices. First on lines 1-6, write in **hiragana** how much it would cost to buy the numbered quantities. Then on line 7, write the total cost of buying the items on lines 1–6.

Items	Prices
1 pencil	¥15
1 tomato	¥60
1 fish	¥230
1 bottle of beer	¥240
1 sweater	¥5,800
25 paper plates (かみの　おさら)	¥229
1 head of lettuce	¥130

■ 6 pencils   <u>きゅうじゅうえん</u>

1. 3 tomatoes   _____

2. 5 fish   _____

3. 12 bottles of beer   _____

4. 2 sweaters _____

5. 2 heads of lettuce _____

6. 50 paper plates _____

7. Total cost _____

B. Look at the following hotel directory and write in Japanese your answer to each of the following questions about floor levels. Write numbers in **hiragana.**

■ A: サウナは　なんかいに　ありますか。

B: 四階に　あります。

30F	とくべつしつ (Suites)
29F	レストラン
5F – 28F	Guest Rooms
4F	サウナ (Sauna)
3F	プール (Pool)
2F	きっさてん
1F	バー (Bar)
B1	はなや (Flower Shop)

1. A: すみません、レストランは　どこに　ありますか。

B. _____

2. A: すみません、この　たてものに　バーが　ありますか。

B: ええ、ありますよ。_____

3. A: すみません、プールは　なんかいに　ありますか。

B: _____

4. A: きっさてんは　どこに　ありますか。

B: _____

5. A: すみません、サウナは　どこに　ありますか。

    B: _____

6. A: この　ホテルの　中に　はなやが　ありますか。

    B: _____

V. Abbreviating verbal expressions, using です

Write your answer to each of the following questions, using です wherever you can.
Wherever you cannot answer with です, write: not possible.

■ あさ　なにを　たべましたか。

  <u>たまごです。</u>

1. あさごはんを　たべましたか。

  _____

2. なんで　がっこうに　きますか。

  _____

3. どんな　おんがくを　よく　ききますか。

  _____

4. なにを　するのが　きらいですか。

  _____

5. どこから　きましたか。

  _____

6. たいてい　なんじに　ねますか。

  _____

7. だれと　よく　でんわで　はなしますか。

  _____

8. あしたも　しゅくだいが　ありますか。

_____

そうごうれんしゅう

You are at a department store and would like to buy an overnight bag. Complete the following conversations with appropriate phrases and sentences, using your imagination.

あんないしょで (At the information desk)

You:　　　_____

あんないがかり
(Information desk clerk):　かばんうりばは　この　おく (back there) に　ございます。

かばんうりばで

You:　　　_____

てんいん
(Salesperson):　　はい、いらっしゃいませ。

You:　　　_____

てんいん:　　この　くろい　かばんは　いかがですか。

You:　　　_____

てんいん:　　３６，０００えんで　ございます。

You:　　　_____

てんいん:　　じゃあ、この　ちゃいろいのは　いかがですか。

You:　　　_____

てんいん:　　３２，０００えんで　ございます。

You:　　　_____

てんいん:　　はい、ありがとう　ございます。おくりものですか。

You:　　　_____

てんいん:　　かしこまりました。

かく　れんしゅう

A. Look at the charts on pages 267–269 of your textbook and write each **kanji** ten times following the correct stroke order.

一									
二									
三									
四									
五									
六									
七									
八									
九									
十									
百									
千									
万									
円									

B. Complete each of the following sentences by finding the items in the illustrations that correspond to the prices listed. Follow the example.

■ <u>えんぴつは</u>　十五円です。

■

¥15

¥630

¥22000

ごじゅうえん

ななせん
さんびゃく
えん

さんぜんろっぴゃくじゅうえん

¥18700

¥2490

にせんはっぴゃくごじゅうえん

きゅうひゃくえん

1. _____ は　一万八千七百円です。

2. _____ は　二万二千円です。

3. _____ は　六百三十円です。

4. _____ は　二千四百九十円です。

C. Look again at the illustrations in exercise B and write the price of each of the following items in **kanji**. Follow the example.

■ けしゴムは　<u>五十円</u>です。

1. とけいは _____ です。

2. かさは _____ です。

3. くつは _____ です。

4. ほんは _____ です。

だい九か
レストランとしょうたい
(Restaurants and Invitations)

I. Deciding on something, using ～に　します, and making a request, using ～を　おねがいします

A. Complete the following conversations, using ～に　します and ～を　おねがいします.

■　1 A-lunch

A: いらっしゃいませ。　ごちゅうもんは。

B: <u>Aランチを　ひとつ　おねがいします。</u>

A: はい、かしこまりました。

1. A: 　　　　　何を　のみますか。
^{なに}

　　B: _____

　　A: そうですか。　じゃあ　私も　こうちゃに　します。

　　ウェイトレス: ごちゅうもんは。

　　B: あのう、すみません。

　　_____

　　ウェイトレス: はい、かしこまりました。

2. A: 　　　　　何を　たべましょうか。
^{なに}

　　B: _____

　　A: わしょくですか。　いいですよ。

3. 　　さしみ
　　A: 　　　何を　たべますか。
^{なに}

　　B: _____

　　A: そうですか。　私は　そばに　します。のみものは？

B: _____

A: 　　　　　　じゃあ、私も　ビールを　ちゅうもんします。

ウェイトレス: ごちゅうもんは。

B: _____

ウェイトレス: はい、かしこまりました。

B. Complete the following conversation between 山川さん and 大木さん by writing the correct particle in each blank.

山川： 　　　　ばんごはんを　たべませんか。

大木： 　　　　ええ、たべましょう。　何_____ (1)　たべましょうか。

山川： 　　　　イタリアりょうり_____ (2)　どうですか。

大木： 　　　　いいですね。　どこ_____ (3)　いきましょうか。

山川： 　　　　あの　レストラン_____ (4)　しましょう。

（レストランで）

山川： 　　　　何_____ (5)　しますか。

大木： 　　　　ぼくは　スパゲティ_____ (6)　します。

山川： 　　　　じゃ、　私は　ピザ_____ (7)　たべます。

大木： 　　　　（ウェイターに）すみません、スパゲティ_____ (8)　ひとつ

　　　　　　　　_____ (9)　ピザ_____ (10)　ひとつ　おねがいします。

II. Inviting and responding, using ～ませんか, ～ましょうか, and ～ましょう

A. Write the correct particle for each verb, as well as an appropriate noun in the left column. Then rewrite each sentence as an invitation.

Noun	Particle	～ませんか
■ ケーキ	__を__ たべる	ケーキを　たべませんか
1.	_____ みる	
2.	_____ きく	
3.	_____ する	
4.	_____ よぶ	
5.	_____ いく	
6.	_____ あそぶ	
7.	_____ あう	

B. Complete the following conversation between すずきさん and さとうさん by writing the appropriate particles and verb forms in the blanks.

すずき：　さとうさん、月曜日_{げつようび}__に__　いっしょに　しょくじ_____

_____ (1)。

さとう：　ええ、ぜひ。何_{なに}_____　_____ (2)。

すずき：　フランスりょうりは　どうですか。

さとう：　いいですね。何時_{なんじ}_____　_____ (3)。

すずき：　六時_じごろは　_____ (4)。

さとう：　ええ、いいですよ。じゃあ、六時_じに　_____ (5)。

III. Expressing purpose, using verb stem 〜に　いきます／きます／かえります

A. Combine the two sentences in each item, using the verb stem 〜に.

■ レストランに　いきます。レストランで　ばんごはんを　たべます。
　　レストランに　ばんごはんを　たべに　いきます。

1. とうきょうに　いきます。とうきょうで　ともだちに　あいます。

　　_____

2. デパートに　いきます。デパートで　かいものを　します。

　　_____

3. アパートに　かえります。アパートで　ねます。

　　_____

4. しょくどうに　いきます。ひるごはんを　たべます。

　　_____

5. としょかんに　いきます。としょかんで　しんぶんを　よみます。

　　_____

6. シカゴに　いきます。シカゴで　えいがを　みます。

　　_____

B. Write your answer to each of the following questions, using verb stem 〜に　いきます.

■ なつやすみ (summer vacation) に　どこに　いきますか。
　そこで　何（なに）を　しますか。
　なつやすみに　ニューヨークに　ともだちに　あいに　いきます。

1. ふゆやすみ (winter vacation) に　どこに　いきますか。そこで　何（なに）を
　しますか。

　　_____

2. はるやすみ (spring break) に　どこに　いきますか。そこで　何を
しますか。

_____

3. なつやすみ (summer vacation) に　どこに　いきますか。そこで　何を
しますか。

_____

4. 週末に　どこに　よく　いきますか。そこで　何を　しますか。

_____

IV. Using a question word + か + (particle)

Complete each of the following dialogues, using either question word + particle or question word + か + (particle).

■ A: __何か__ たべませんか。
   なに

  B: ええ、いいですね。ピザは　どうですか。

1. A: 土曜日に _____
   どようび

  B: ええ、かいものに　いきましたよ。

  A: そうですか。 _____ いきましたか。

  B: えきの　ちかくの　デパートに　いきました。

2. A: きのうの　ばん、_____ うちに　きましたか。

  B: はい、きました。田中さんが　きましたよ。

3. A: 山田さん、　私の　ねこを _____ みましたか。

  B: ええ、みましたよ。

  A: そうですか。 _____ みましたか。

  B: つくえの　下に　いましたよ。

4. A: さとうさんは _____ 日本に　かえりますか。

  B: ふゆやすみ (winter break) に　かえります。

  A: いいですね。

  B: ブラウンさんも _____ 日本に　きて下さいね。

V. Talking about activities and events, using ～で　～が　あります

Fill in the blanks with the particle で or に.

1. A: 今週の　金曜日に　コンサートが　あります。

   B: どこ_____　ありますか。

   A: こうえん_____　あります。

2. A: どこか_____　いい　きっさてんが　ありますか。

   B: ええ、ありますよ。　あそこ_____　あります。

3. A: 先生、かいわ (conversation) の　テストは　どこ_____　ありますか。

   B: 私の　けんきゅうしつ_____　あります。

4. A: その　えいがは　どこ_____　ありますか。

   B: 学生会館_____　あります。

5. A: 田中さんの　コートは　どこ_____　ありますか。

   B: たんすの　中_____　あります。

そうごうれんしゅう

Kimura-san makes a telephone call to the Suzukis and Mrs. Suzuki answers the phone. The following sentences from their conversation are scrambled. Figure out the correct sequence and number the sentences accordingly.

木村

_____ もしもし、すずきさんの　おたくですか。

_____ ぼく、じょうとうだいがくの　木村ですが、アリスさんは　いらっしゃいますか。

すずき

_____ はい、いますよ。ちょっと　まって下さい。アリスさん、でんわですよ。

_____ はい、そうです。

After Mrs. Suzuki, Alice comes to the phone. Kimura-san wants to take her for a drive sometime this weekend. Figure out the correct sequence and number the sentences.

アリス

__1__ はい、アリスです。

_____ いいえ、日曜日は　いそがしくありません。

_____ じゃあ、おねがいします。どうも　ありがとう。

_____ 十時ですね。いいですよ。

_____ ああ、木村さん、こんばんは。

_____ ああ、いいですね。　いきましょう。　何時ごろ　いきましょうか。

木村

_____ あのう、アリスさんは　今週の　日曜日は　いそがしいですか。

_____ じゃあ、十時に　アリスさんの　うちに　いきます。

_____ いっしょに　ドライブに　いきませんか。

_____ 十時ごろは　どうですか。

__2__ あっ、アリスさん。木村です。こんばんは。

かく　れんしゅう

A. Look at the charts on pages 301–303 of your textbook and write each **kanji** ten times, following the correct stroke order.

月										
火										
水										
木										
金										
土										
曜										
年										
時										
間										
週										
何										
半										
分										
今										

B. Rewrite each sentence using the **kanji** you have learned. The number in parentheses indicates the number of **kanji** you should use.

1. じゅぎょうは　げつようびと　すいようびと　きんようびに　あります。(9)

   _____

2. こんしゅうの　かようびと　もくようびは　いそがしいです。(8)

   _____

3. たなかさんは　なんねんせいですか。(5)

   _____

4. どようびの　よじはんに　がくせいかいかんで　あいましょう。(8)

   _____

5. にじかんはんぐらい　ねました。(4)

   _____

6. にほんごの　じゅぎょうは　じゅうじじゅうごふんに　あります。(7)

   _____

第十課
だい か

私の家族　(My Family)
かぞく

I. Counting people, using 人; counting age, using さい; expressing the order within a family,
にん
using 番(目).
ばん め

A. Look at the family tree. You are Mr. Ken'ichi Suzuki. Answer each question.

鈴木けんいちさんの　家族
すずき　　　　　　　　　　かぞく

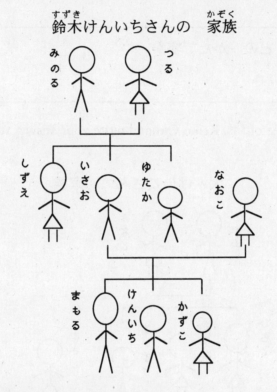

■ 鈴木　いさおさんは　どのかたですか。
　すずき

　　いさおは　私の　父です。
　　　　　　　　　ちち

1. まもるさんは　どの　かたですか。

_____

2. なおこさんは　どの　かたですか。

_____

3. つるさんは　どのかたですか。

_____

4. かずこさんは　どの　かたですか。

_____

5. みのるさんは　どの　かたですか。

_____

6. しずえさんは　どの　かたですか。

_____

B. Look at the family tree of Ms. Keiko Ōki and write your answer to each of the following questions.

大木けいこさんの　家族

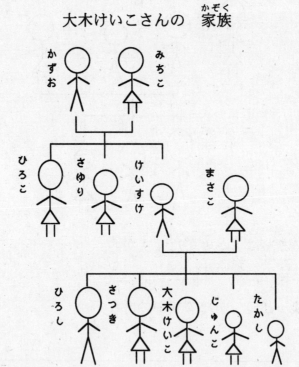

■　大木　じゅんこさんは　どの　かたですか。
　　じゅんこさんは　けいこさんの　妹さんです。

1. 大木ひろしさんは　どの　かたですか。

    _____

2. 大木まさこさんは　どの　かたですか。

    _____

3. 大木さつきさんは　どの　かたですか。

    _____

4. 大木たかしさんは　どの　かたですか。

    _____

5. 大木みちこさんは　どの　かたですか。

    _____

6. 大木さゆりさんは　どの　かたですか。

    _____

C. 日本語で こたえてください。すうじ (number) を　ひらがなで　かいてください。そして、かんじも　下に　かいてください。(To answer the following questions, you may need to look again at the family trees of Ken'ichi Taguchi, on page 93, and of Keiko Ōki, on page 94.)

■ 大木　じゅん子さんは　何番目ですか。

　　したから　にばんめです。
　　　下　　　二　番　目

1. 田口さんの　ご家族は　何人家族ですか。 　　_____

2. 田口　かず子さんは　ご兄弟が　何人いますか。 　　_____

3. 田口　けんいちさんは　何番目ですか。 　　_____

4. 田口　かず子さんは　何番目ですか。 　　_____

5. 大木さんの　ご家族は　何人家族ですか。 　　_____

6. 大木けい子さんは　ご兄弟が　何人　いますか。 　　_____

II. Describing a resultant state, using verb て-form ＋ いる

A. First look at the following picture. Then complete each of the following sentences by choosing the appropriate particle and verb.

マクニール
イギリス人
コンピュータの
かいしゃ

フランソワ
フランス人
モデル (model)

スコット
アメリカ人
大学生

ルチアーノ
イタリア人
くつの　かいしゃ

コール
ドイツ人
大学院生
いん

ジャイシュリー
インド人
大学の　先生

チャン
ちゅうごく人
大学生

リー
かんこく人
くるまの　かいしゃ

■ コールさんは　めがね__を__　__かけていません__。スコットさん__も__ __かけていません__。

フランソワさんは　ハイヒール (high heel)　__を__　__はいています__。
ズボン__も__　__はいています__。

1. マクニールさんは　スーツ_____　_____。

2. スコットさんは　ジーパン_____　_____。

3. リーさんは　イヤリング_____　_____。

4. ジャイシュリーさんは　スカート_____　_____が、

チャンさんは　スカート_____　_____。

5. フランソワさんは　ズボン_____　_____。

めがね_____　_____。

6. マクニールさんは　コンピュータの　かいしゃ_____

_____が、スコットさんは　かいしゃ_____

_____。

B. Your friend is meeting the people listed below for the first time in a hotel lobby. Give your friend a description, in writing, of each person in terms of clothing and physical appearance.

■ マクニールさん

マクニールさんは　スーツを　きていて、めがねを　かけています。
せが　あまり　高たかくありません。　ゆびわは　していません。
ネックレスも　していません。

1. コールさん

_____

_____

_____

2. ジャイシュリーさん

_____

_____

_____

3. ルチアーノさん

_____

_____

_____

III. Describing physical appearance and skills, using 〜は 〜が

A. Look again at the illustrations on page 96. Fill in the blanks with the appropriate particle and adjective or verb.

■ マクニールさん＿は＿ かお＿が＿ あまり ＿まるくありません。

1. ジャイ・シュリーさん_____ かみ_____ _____。

2. ルチアーノさん_____ 目^め_____ _____。

3. チャンさん_____ 口^{くち}_____ _____。

4. スコットさん_____ せ_____ とても_____。

5. ルチアーノさん_____ かみ_____ あまり_____。

6. リーさん_____ かお_____ _____。

7. フランソワさん_____ フランスご_____ _____。

B. Look again at the illustrations on page 96. Write a sentence comparing each of the follow-ing pairs of people in terms of the feature in parentheses.

■ リーさん　スコットさん　（せ）
　<u>リーさんは　せが　ひくいですが、スコットさんは　せが　たかいです。</u>

　スコットさん　コールさん　（せ）
　<u>スコットさんは　せが　たかいです。コールさんも　せが　たかいです。</u>

1. マクニールさん　ルチアーノさん　（かみ）

　_____

2. ジャイシュリーさん　チャンさん　（目）

　_____

3. フランソワさん　チャンさん　（めがね）

　_____

4. コールさん　リーさん　（スーツ）

　_____

5. チャンさん　リーさん　（ズボン）

　_____

6. コールさん　ルチアーノさん　（せ）

　_____

IV. Connecting phrases, using the verb and adjective て-forms

A. Write your answer to each of the following questions, using the て-form and the cues in parentheses.

■ お父さんは　どんな　かたですか。(physical appearance／せいかく)

　父は　せが　たかくて　やさしいです。

1. 日本語の　先生は　どんな　かたですか。　(nationality／せいかく)

_____

2. お母さんは　どんな　かたですか。(せいかく／physical appearance)

　かあ

_____

3. 一番　いい　ともだちは　どんな　人ですか。(せいかく／skills)

　ばん

_____

4. お父さんは　どんな　かたですか。(occupation／skills)

　とう

_____

5. おばあさんは　どんな　かたですか。(physical appearance／せいかく)

_____

B. Write a description of a close friend in terms of physical features or clothing, personality, and skills. Try to use the て-form 〜が (*but*) and も (*also*) as necessary.

■

　私の　一番　いい　ともだちは　山田たかしさんです。山田さんは

　　　いちばん

せが　たかくて、とても　かっこいい (good-looking) です。そして、

えいごが　とても　上手です。あたまも　とても　いいです。　山田さんは

　　　　　　じょうず

たいてい　ジーンズを　はいていて、Tシャツを　きています。

_____

_____

_____

_____

V. Describing people and things, using nouns and modifying clauses

A. Look again at the illustrations on page 96. Write your answer to each of the following questions, using noun modification.

■ マクニールさんは　どの　人ですか。

　スーツを　きている　イギリス人の　男の人です。

1. フランソワさんは　どの　人ですか。

_____

2. リーさんは　どの　人ですか。

_____

3. ルチアーノさんは　どの　人ですか。

_____

4. コールさんは　どの　人ですか。

_____

5. ジャイシュリーさんは　どの　人ですか。

_____

B. Draw a picture of your family and write a description of each member of your family, using nouns and modifying clauses.

■ この　せが　ひくくて　すこし　ふとっている　人は　私の　父です。

_____

_____

_____

_____

_____

_____

_____

そうごうれんしゅう
総合練習

Tom-san and Hiroshi-san are talking about the following snapshot of Tom's family. Fill in the blanks with the appropriate words.

ひろし： あっ、おもしろい しゃしんですね。りょこう＿＿＿＿(1)

　　　　 ときの しゃしんですか。

トム： ええ、きょねん フロリダ＿＿＿＿(2) いきました。

ひろし： いいですね。この 男の人は ＿＿＿＿＿＿＿＿(3) ですか。

　　　　 とても 大きい さかなですね。

トム： ええ、それは 私の 父です。父は さかなを つる (fishing) のが

_____ (4)、この 日は たくさん つりました。

ひろし： そうですか。よかったですね。じゃあ、この ぼうしを

_____ (5) 人は トムさんの お母さんですか。

トム： ええ、_____ (6) は うみ (sea) _____ (7) たいてい

ぼうしを _____ (8)。そして、サングラスも

_____ (9)。

ひろし： そうですか。この 男の子は。

トム： これは 私の 弟の ボブです。 ボブは げんきで とても

いい子です_____ (10)、べんきょう_____ (11) あまり

すきじゃありません。

ひろし： でも、目が _____ (12) はなが

_____ (13)、 とても かわいいですね。

トム： そうかなあ。

A. Look at the charts on pages 341–343 of your textbook and write each **kanji** ten times, following the correct stroke order.

男										
女										
子										
目										
耳										
口										
足										
手										
父										
母										
兄										
姉										
弟										
妹										
家										
族										

B. Rewrite each sentence, using all the **kanji** you have learned. The number in parentheses indicates the number of **kanji** you should use.

1. たなかさんの　ごきょうだいは　なんにん　いますか。(6)

_____

2. やまださんの　おにいさんと　おねえさんは　めが　きれいですね。(5)

_____

3. おとうさんと　おかあさんは　いま　どこに　いますか。(3)

_____

4. いもうとは　かようびに　ここに　きます。(4)

_____

5. その　おとこのこは　わたしの　おとうとで、しょうがくせいです。(7)

_____

6. わたしは　あねが　ひとり　いて　あにが　ふたり　います。(7)

_____

7. ちちと　ははは　にほんに　すんでいます。(4)

_____

8. あねは　てと　あしが　とても　ながいです。(3)

_____

第十一課
おもいで (Memories)

I. **Talking about time, using nouns/adjectives + 時, ～月, ～日, ～か月, and duration + まえ (に)**

A. Write the following dates in **hiragana** and in **kanji**.

■ 4/10 　　しがつ　とおか　四月十日

1. 1/15 _____ 　　6. 9/1 _____

2. 2/3 _____ 　　7. 12/8 _____

3. 3/20 _____ 　　8. 8/14 _____

4. 7/6 _____ 　　9. 6/2 _____

5. 10/7 _____ 　　10. 4/9 _____

B. Fill in each blank with the correct date spelled in **hiragana** and in **kanji**, except for years in the Gregorian calendar, such as 1996.

■ きょうは　さんがつじゅうよっかです。　三月十四日です。

　　めいじ一年は　せんはっぴゃくろくじゅうはちねんです。　１８６８年です。

1. きょうは_____。

2. きのうは_____。

3. あしたは_____。

4. 私の誕生日は_____。

5. クリスマスは_____。

6. アメリカのどくりつきねんび (Independence Day)は _____。

7. しょうわ二十年は _____。

8. 五年まえは _____。

9. 今年（ことし）は _____。

C. しつもんに 日本語（ご）で こたえて下さい。

1. なつやすみは 何か月（げつ）ぐらい ありますか。

    _____

2. 去年（きょ）の クリスマスの時 どこに 行（い）きましたか。そこに 何日（なんにち）ぐらい
   いましたか。

    _____

3. この大学に どのくらい いますか。

    _____

4. 一がっき (one term/semester/quarter) は 何か月（げつ） ありますか。

    _____

5. 誕生日（たんじょう）は 何か月（げつ）まえでしたか。

    _____

II. Talking about past experiences, using verb た ことがある; listing representative activities, using verb たり verb たりする

A. Write a sentence for each of the following saying whether you have or have never done each of the following activities.

■ スペインに 行く

　スペインに 行ったことが あります。 or

　スペインに 行ったことが ありません。

1. きものを きる

_____

2. ひこうきに　のる

_____

3. たばこを　すう

_____

4. つりを　する

_____

5. 富士山(Mt. Fuji)に　のぼる

_____

6. こうつうじこに　あう

_____

B. You are looking for a pen pal through a computer network. Ask five questions about activities that the person may or may not have done before.

■ <u>スキーを　した　ことが　ありますか。</u>

1. _____

2. _____

3. _____

4. _____

5. _____

C. Complete each of the following sentences, using 〜たり，〜たりする.

■ A: あさ　たいてい　何を　しますか。
　　B: そうですね。新聞を　__読んだり__　ラジオを　__聞いたり__　します。

1. A: ひまな　時、よく　何を　しますか。

　　B: そうですね。　たいてい　テレビを　_____　本を

　　　_____　しますね。

2. A: 高校の　時、どんな　ことを　よく　しましたか。

　　B: そうですね。　デートを　_____　フットボールを

　　見に　_____　しました。

3. A: はるやすみに　どこかに　行きますか。

　　B: ええ、ともだちの　家に　あそびに　行きます。　ともだちと　おさけを

　　　_____おいしいものを　_____　します。

4. A: 週末に　どんな　ことを　しましたか。

　　B: そうじを　_____　せんたくを　_____

　　しました。

5. A: 田中先生は　ふゆやすみにも　しごとが　たくさん　ありますか。

　　B: ええ、しけんを　_____　レポートを

　　　_____　するから　とても　いそがしいんですよ。

D. Write your answer to each of the following questions, using ～たり，～たりする.

■ 小さい 時に よく 何を して あそびましたか。
　<u>ファミコンを　したり　こうえんで　あそんだり　しました。</u>

1. 小さい 時に よく どんな ことを して あそびましたか。

　　_____

2. ひとりで さびしい 時に 何をしますか。

　　_____

3. やすみに 家族と どんな ことを しますか。

　　_____

4. 去^{きょ}年の ふゆやすみに どんな ことを しましたか。

　　_____

5. ひまな 時^{とき}、何を しますか。

　　_____

III. Expressing reasons, using the plain past form of verbs and adjectives + んです and the plain form of verbs and adjectives + からです

A. Complete the following chart.

Plain Present Affirmative (dictionary form)	Plain Present Negative Form	Plain Past Affirmative Form	Plain Past Negative Form
おきる	おきない	おきた	おきなかった
1. せんたくする			
2. 食べる			
3. 飲む			
4. 行く			
5. 見る			
6. あそぶ			
7. 聞く			
8. すう			
9. つくる			
10. ある			
11. 来る			

B. Complete the following chart.

Plain Present Affirmative Form	Plain Present Negative Form	Plain Past Affirmative Form	Plain Past Negative Form
しろい	しろくない	しろかった	しろくなかった
1. たいへん			
2. あかるい			
3. いい			
4. しずか			
5. たのしい			
6. すてき			
7. きれい			
8. ひろい			

C. Write your answer to each of the following questions, using 〜からです and 〜んです.

■ こうこうの時、何をよくしましたか。 どうしてですか。

　　よく山に　行きました。キャンプをするのがすきだったからです。／
すきだったんです。

1. どうして　日本語を　べんきょうするんですか。

_____

_____

2. どうして　この　大学に　来たんですか。

_____

_____

3. 子供の　時、よく　何を　しましたか。どうしてですか。

（こども）

_____

_____

4. 子供の　時、何が　きらいでしたか。どうしてですか。

（こども）

_____

_____

5. 日本語の　クラスは　どうですか。どうしてですか。

（ご）

_____

_____

IV. Expressing hearsay, using the plain form of verbs/adjectives/the copula + そうです

A. Read the following paragraph. Write sentences that report what you have read, using そうです of hearsay.

ことばのリスト：　しんでしまう　to die

　　小さい時、私の　家には　大きい　いぬが　いました。なまえは
ポチでした。私は　ポチが　とても　すきでしたから、よく　いっしょに　山に
行ったり、ともだちの　家に　あそびに　行ったり　しました。旅行の　時も
ポチは　いっしょに　来ました。小学校の　六年生の　時に　ポチは
こうつうじこに　あって、しんでしまいました。とても　かなしかったから、
なきました。

この　人の　家には　大きい　いぬが　いた　そうです。 _____

_____

_____

_____

_____

V. Using noun-modifying clauses in the past and present

A. Write a question that fits each of the following answers.

■ スミスさんは　きのう　<u>その　レストランに</u>　行きました。

A: <u>きのう　スミスさんが　行った　レストラン</u>　は　どんな　レストラン
でしたか。

B: わしょくの　レストランです。

1. きのう　パーティーで　<u>その　人</u>に　会いました。

A: _____は　どんな　人でしたか。

B: せが　とても　たかい　人でした。

2. 子供の　時、<u>それを</u>　あまり　食べませんでした。(Hint: Use もの.)

A: _____は　何ですか。

B: たまごです。

3. お母さんは　去年　<u>その　くるまを</u>　買いました。

A: _____は　どんな　くるまですか。

B: トヨタです。

4. 中学の　時、<u>その　おんがくを</u>　よく　聞きました。

A: _____は　どんな　おんがくですか。

B: ロックです。

5. 妹さんは　子供の　時　その人が　すきでした。

A: _____は　どの人ですか。

B: 山田さんです。

6. 子供の　時　その　人は　やせていました。

A: _____は　だれですか。

B: リーさんです。

B. Write a short paragraph that compares your childhood and adult habits, using the cues.

■ 私／食べる／もの

私が　小さい　時　よく　食べた　ものは　りんごです。あまり
食べなかった　ものは　レタスです。今、よく　食べる　ものは　やさいや
くだものです。そして、今　あまり　食べない　ものは　にくです。

1. 私／すき／おんがく

　_____

　_____

2. 行く／ところ

　_____

　_____

3. 見る／テレビ

　_____

　_____

4. きらい／スポーツ

_____

_____

総合練習
そうごうれんしゅう

Write two short paragraphs describing the best and the worst trips you ever took. (一番_{ばん}
いい 旅行_{りょこう}と 一番_{ばん} ひどい 旅行_{りょこう}) Try to use different expressions you have learned
so far. It's alright to make some mistakes. Using transition words from the following list
will help create a flow in your composition.

Conjunctions

そして	and	そのあとで	after that
それから	and then	そのとき	at that time
でも	but	ですから	therefore

■ 私は ニューヨークに 行った_い ことが あります。1988年の

なつでした。とても たのしい 旅行_{りょこう}でした。ニューヨークでは

買いもの_いに 行ったり、ミュージカル (musical) を 見たり しました。...

それから....。そのあとで... でも 去年の ロサンゼルスの 旅行_{りょこう}は

ひどかったんです。その ときは...

_____

_____

_____

_____

_____

_____

書く練習<ruby>練習<rt>れんしゅう</rt></ruby>

A. Look at the charts on pages 383–385 of your textbook and write each **kanji** ten times, following the correct stroke order.

行									
来									
帰									
食									
飲									
見									
聞									
読									
書									
話									
高									
校									
出									

会										
買										

B. Rewrite each sentence using all the **kanji** you have learned. The number in parentheses indicates the number of **kanji** you should use.

1. ちゅうがくの　ときの　ともだちに　あいました。(4)

   _____

2. ばんごはんを　たべに　きませんか。(2)

   _____

3. わたしは　こうこうの　とき　よく　ほんを　よんだり、てがみを
   かいたり　しました。(7)

   _____

4. きのう　くつを　かいに　デパートに　いきました。(2)

   _____

5. パーティに　いって、たべたり、のんだり、ともだちと　はなしを
   したり　しました。(4)

   _____

6. きのうは　くじごろ　うちに　かえって、じゅうじまで　テレビを
   みて　ねました。(7)

   _____

7. きのうの　あさ　はちじに　おきて、すきな　おんがくを　きいて、
   くじごろ　でかけました。(6)

   _____

第十二課
病気 (Health)
びょうき

I. Expressing capability, using potential forms of verbs

A. Fill in the following charts.

	Potential Form		Potential Form
食べる	食べられる	5. 読む	
1. おきる		6. 話す	
2. 飲む		7. 行く	
3. ねる		8. 来る	
4. 書く		9. する	

	Present		Past		て-form
	Affirmative	Negative	Affirmative	Negative	
食べる	食べられる	食べられない	食べられた	食べられなかった	食べられて
10. つくる					
11. いる					
12. 来る					
13. する					

B. Fill in the blanks with the appropriate particles and the potential form of verbs.

■ A: このかんじ__が__　読めますか。
　　　　　　　　　　読む
　 B: いいえ、読めません。

1. A: あした　九時_____　_____。
　　　　　　　　　　　　　　　　　　来る

　 B: はい。

2. A: 山田さんは　テニス_____　_____。
　　　　　　　　　　　　　　　　　　　　する

　 B: いいえ、_____。

3. A: おさけ_____ _____。
                              飲む

   B: ええ、すこし _____。

4. A: すし_____ _____。
                              食べる

   B: はい、とても 好〈す〉きです。

5. A: きのう さとうさん_____ _____。
                                          会う

   B: いいえ、_____。

6. A: 日本語〈ご〉_____ 手紙〈てがみ〉_____ _____。
                                                  書く

   B: ええ、すこし _____。

C. Describe what each of your family members can or cannot do. Try to use different verbs
   for each description.

   ■ 私の父は ゴルフが 出来〈でき〉ます。でも、スキーは 出来〈でき〉ません。

   1. _____

   2. _____

   3. _____

II. Expressing cause, using the て-form of adjectives, verbs, and copula です

A. Look at the following illustrations and complete each of the dialogues, using appropriate phrases for cause and effect.

■   1.   2.   3.

4.   5.   6.   7.

■ A: どうしましたか。

    B: <u>あたまが　いたくて　べんきょう出来ないんです。</u>

1. A: どうしたんですか。

    B: _____。

2. A: どうしましたか。

    B: _____。

3. A: かおが　あかいですね。　どうしたんですか。

    B: _____。

4. A: どうしたんですか。

    B: _____。

5. A: どうしたんですか。

    B: _____。

6. A: どうしたんですか。あまり　食べませんね。

    B: _____。

7. A: どうしたんですか。

B: _____。

III. Expressing desire, using verb stem + たい and たがる

A. Look at the chart indicating your and Tanaka-san's wishes. はい means that the activity in the left column is agreeable, and いいえ means that the activity is not agreeable. Write sentences about what you and Tanaka-san do or do not want to do.

		私	田中さん
■	家に　帰る	はい	はい
1	およぐ	いいえ	いいえ
2	しゃしんを　とる	はい	いいえ
3	ねつを　はかる	いいえ	はい
4	あるく	はい	はい
5	やきゅうを　する	はい	いいえ
6	日本語で　話す	いいえ	はい

■ <u>私は　家に　帰りたいです。田中さんも　家に　帰りたがっています。</u>

1. _____

   _____

2. _____

   _____

3. _____

   _____

4. _____

   _____

5. _____

_____

6. _____

_____

B. Write five sentences about what you and each of your family members want to do.

■ 私は　アイスクリームが　食べたいです。

父は　ゴルフに　行きたがっています。

1. _____

2. _____

3. _____

4. _____

5. _____

IV. Giving suggestions, using verb たら　どうですか and ほうが　いいです

A. Each of the following people has a problem. Give suggestions or advice, using verb 〜たら
どうですか, 〜たほうが　いいですよ, and 〜ないほうが　いいですよ.

■ かんじが　むずかしくて　よく　わからないんです。

　かんじの　じしょを　買ったら　どうですか。

　先生と　話した　ほうが　いいですよ。

　じゅぎょうを　休まない　ほうが　いいですよ。

1. 好きな人がいるんです。

_____

_____

_____

2. とても　ふとったんです。

_____

_____

_____

3. のどが　いたいんです。

_____

_____

_____

4. こしが　いたいんです。

_____

_____

_____

5. 今、お金が　ないんです。

_____

_____

_____

B. Complete the following conversations, using verb 〜たら　どうですか or 〜た／ない
ほうが　いいですよ.

1. 山本(やまもと):　本田(ほんだ)さん、どうしたんですか。
   本田(ほんだ):　おさけを　飲んで、ちょっと　気分(きぶん)が　わるいんです。

   山本(やまもと):　そうですか。　おさけは　あまり _____。

　　　水を　_____。

<ruby>本田<rt>ほんだ</rt></ruby>:　そうですね。すみませんが、お水を　下さい。

2.　田中:　先生、どうですか。

　　いしゃ:　ちょっと　ねつが　ありますね。それに、いが　だいぶ　よわって

　　　　　　いますね。(Your stomach has weakened considerably.)

　　田中:　学校が　いそがしくて　あまり　休めなかったんです。

　　いしゃ:　あまり　_____。

　　　　　　よく　_____。

　　田中:　はい。

V. Asking for and giving permission, using verb てもいい　ですか or verb てもいい でしょうか。

A. Fill in the blanks with appropriate phrases to ask for permission. Choose the correct degree of politeness depending on the situation.

■ A: 山田さん、この本を　<u>読んでも　いいですか</u>。

B: はい、どうぞ。

1. スミス: 山本さん、えいごで _____。

　　山本:　　Sure. What would you like to talk about?

2. 学生:　　先生、ひらがなで_____。

　　先生:　　いいえ。　かんじで　書いて下さい。

3. 山本:　　スミスさん、たばこを _____。

　　スミス: すみません。ちょっと　こまるんですが。

4 田中:　　山本さん、あした　あそびに_____。

　　山本:　　ええ、どうぞ。何時に　来ますか。

5. 学生:　　先生、しゅくだいを　月曜日に _____。

　　先生:　　いいえ、あした　出して下さい。

6. 山下：　先生、コーヒーを_____。

いしゃ：そうですね。コーヒーは　いいですよ。でも、おさけは　飲まない
　　　　　ほうが　いいですね。

B. Ask each of the following people for permission.

■ 先生

　しゅくだいを　あした　出しても　いいでしょうか。

1. ルームメート

_____

2. クラスメート

_____

3. 一番_{ばん}　いい　ともだち

_____

4. いしゃ

_____

5. あなたの　お父さん

_____

6. あなたの　お母さん

_____

Complete the following conversation, using appropriate phrases.

スミスさん

本田:　　　スミスさん、どうしたんですか。

スミス:　　_____、_____んです。

本田:　　　こまりましたね。いしゃ_____　_____
　　　　　　どうですか。

スミス:　　ええ、きょう　行きます。

スミスさんは　病院に　います。

いしゃ:　　どうしましたか。

スミス:　　_____んです。

いしゃ:　　そうですか。じゃあ、ちょっと　そこによこに　なって下さい
　　　　　　(Please lie down)。

スミス:　　はい。

いしゃ:　　(Pressing his lower back)ここは　どうですか。

スミス:　　ああっ、　とても_____。

いしゃ:　　ヘルニヤの　ようですね。(It looks like a hernia.)　くわしい
　　　　　　けんさ (detailed examination) をしますから、来週　もう　一度

来てください。それから、薬を　あげますから、いたい　時に
飲んで下さい。

スミス：　　先生、＿＿＿＿＿＿＿＿＿＿いいでしょうか。

いしゃ：　　しごとですか。むりは　＿＿＿＿＿＿＿＿＿ほうが

いいですね。二、三日　家で＿＿＿＿＿＿＿＿＿ほうが
に　さんにち

いいですよ。

スミス：　　はい、わかりました。ありがとうございました。

書く練習
れんしゅう

A. Look at the charts on pages 418–420 of your textbook and write each **kanji** ten times, following the correct stroke order.

元										
気										
入										
薬										
休										
体										
病										
院										
住										
所										

語										
好										
毎										
回										
度										

B. Rewrite each sentence using the **kanji** you have learned. The number in parentheses indicates the number of **kanji** you should use.

1. きのうは　ねつが　３９ど　あったから、にほんごの　クラスを
   やすみました。(5)

   _____

2. せんしゅうは　びょうきで　にゅういんしましたが、いまは　もう
   げんきです。(9)

   _____

3. この　くすりは　まいにち　さんかい　のんでください。(7)

   _____

4. びょういんの　じゅうしょを　かいてください。(6)

   _____

5. わたしは　くすりが　あまり　すきじゃありません。(3)

   _____

LABORATORY
MANUAL

Name _____ Class _____ Date _____

 だいいっか　(Chapter 1)
The Japanese Sound System and Hiragana

I. Introduction and Hiragana あ〜そ

A. Listen to each of the following words or phrases and repeat it. You will then hear the word or phrase again. Write each word or phrase. Stop the tape as necessary.

1. _____   6. _____   11. _____   16. _____

2. _____   7. _____   12. _____   17. _____

3. _____   8. _____   13. _____   18. _____

4. _____   9. _____   14. _____

5. _____   10. _____   15. _____

B. Listen to each of the following words and repeat it, paying attention to the whispered sound.

ki shi
きし　shore   ku ki
くき　stalk   su so
すそ　hem   shi ki
しき　four seasons

ki ku
きく　chrysanthemum   ku sa
くさ　grass   su ki
すき　like   shi ka
しか　deer

C. You are attending an orientation session for international students at a university in Japan. Some of the students approach you and introduce themselves. Following Brown-san's example, greet each person and give your name.

■ You hear:　はじめまして。　かとうです。　どうぞ　よろしく。

　You say:　はじめまして。ブラウンです。どうぞ　よろしく。

Laboratory Manual: Chapter 1 185

II. Hiragana た～ほ

A. Listen to each of the following words or phrases and repeat it. You will then hear the word or phrase again. Write each word or phrase. Stop the tape as necessary.

1. _____	6. _____	11. _____	16. _____
2. _____	7. _____	12. _____	17. _____
3. _____	8. _____	13. _____	18. _____
4. _____	9. _____	14. _____	19. _____
5. _____	10. _____	15. _____	20. _____

B. Listen to each of the following words and repeat it, paying attention to the whispered sound.

tsu chi
つち soil

ka tsu
かつ to win

chi ka
ちか underground

tsu ki
つき moon

ma tsu
まつ to wait for

chi chi
ちち my father

sa chi ko
さちこ Sachiko (female name)

C. You run into some of your classmates and instructors on campus at various times of the day. They greet you. Give each person the appropriate response. You will then hear the correct response.

■ You hear: 9:00 a.m.,
o ha yoo　go za i ma su
おはよう ございます。

You say:
o ha yoo　go za i ma su
おはよう ございます。

You hear:
o ha yoo　go za i ma su
おはよう ございます。

D. You run into some of your classmates and instructors during the day. After hearing the cue telling you the time of day, greet each person. You will then hear the correct greeting.

■ You hear: 3:00 p.m.

You say:
kon' ni chi wa
こんにちは。

You hear:
kon' ni chi wa
こんにちは。

III. Hiragana ま～ん

A. Listen to each of the following words or phrases and repeat it. You will then hear the word or phrase again. Write each word or phrase. Stop the tape as necessary.

1. _____	6. _____	11. _____	16. _____
2. _____	7. _____	12. _____	17. _____
3. _____	8. _____	13. _____	18. _____
4. _____	9. _____	14. _____	
5. _____	10. _____	15. _____	

B. Listen to each of the following words and repeat it, paying attention to the [n] sound. You will then hear the word again.

あに elder brother   あんい easygoing
こな powder   こんな this kind of
この this   こんの of navy blue

C. Your last class is over and you are going home. You see some of your classmates and instructors in the hallway and expect to see them again soon. Listen to each cue identifying a classmate or an instructor and greet that person appropriately. You will then hear the correct greeting.

■ You hear: ya ma da san
             やまださん

You say: jaa   ma ta
           じゃあ、また。

You hear: jaa   ma ta
           じゃあ、また。

Laboratory Manual: Chapter 1

IV. Hiragana が〜ぽ: Voiced consonants

A. Listen to each of the following words or phrases and repeat it. You will then hear the word or phrase again. Write each word or phrase. Stop the tape as necessary.

1. _____ 6. _____ 11. _____ 16. _____

2. _____ 7. _____ 12. _____ 17. _____

3. _____ 8. _____ 13. _____ 18. _____

4. _____ 9. _____ 14. _____

5. _____ 10. _____ 15. _____

B. Listen to each of the following pairs of words and identify which word in the pair has a voiced sound. Circle first or second.

■ first (second)

1. first   second   4. first   second

2. first   second   5. first   second

3. first   second   6. first   second

C. Listen to each of the following phrases and repeat it, paying attention to the length of each sound. You will then hear the phrase again.

D. What would you say in each of the following situations? Listen to each cue identifying a situation and respond appropriately. You will then hear the correct response.

■ You hear: You lost a book you borrowed from a friend.

You say: すみません。

You hear: すみません。

Laboratory Manual: Chapter 1   191

V. Hiragana ああ〜わあ: Long vowels

A. Listen to each of the following words or phrases and repeat it. You will then hear the word or phrase again. Write each word or phrase. Stop the tape as necessary.

1. _____	6. _____	11. _____	16. _____
2. _____	7. _____	12. _____	17. _____
3. _____	8. _____	13. _____	18. _____
4. _____	9. _____	14. _____	19. _____
5. _____	10. _____	15. _____	20. _____

B. Listen to each of the following questions and repeat it, paying attention to the whispered sound.

C. Listen to each of the following pairs of words and repeat it, paying attention to the contrast in pronunciation between each pair.

1. え picture　　　　　　　　　　ええ yes
2. い stomach　　　　　　　　　　いい good
3. いえ house　　　　　　　　　　いいえ no
4. すし sushi　　　　　　　　　　すうじ number expression
5. さと countryside　　　　　　　さこう sugar
6. きれ cloth　　　　　　　　　　きれい pretty, clean
7. くつ shoes　　　　　　　　　　くつう pain
8. かぜ wind　　　　　　　　　　かぜい taxation
9. おばさん aunt　　　　　　　　おばあさん grandmother
10. おじさん uncle　　　　　　　おじいさん grandfather
11. ここ here　　　　　　　　　　こうこう high school
12. しゅじん my husband　　　　しゅうじん prisoner

D. Look at the following drawing. Imagine that you are standing by the window and your friend is at the door. The room has various items and you want to know what they are called in Japanese. Listen to each cue in English and ask your friend what the item is called in Japanese. You will then hear the correct question. Repeat the question.

■ You hear:　window

You say:　これは　にほんごで　なんと　いいますか。

You hear:　これは　にほんごで　なんと　いいますか。

You repeat:　これは　にほんごで　なんと　いいますか。

E. Look again at the drawing in activity D. Listen to each cue in English and ask your friend what the item is called in Japanese. You will then hear the correct question. Repeat the question. You will then hear the answer to the question. Stop the tape and write the Japanese word.

■ You hear:　window

You say:　これは　にほんごで　なんと　いいますか。

You hear:　これは　にほんごで　なんと　いいますか。

You say:　これは　にほんごで　なんと　いいますか。

You hear:　「まど」と　いいます。

You write:　まど

1. _____　　4. _____

2. _____　　5. _____

3. _____　　6. _____

Name _____ Class _____ Date _____

F. Listen to each of the following English words and ask how to say it in Japanese. You will then hear the correct question. Repeat the question. You will then hear the answer to the question. Stop the tape and write the Japanese word.

■ You hear: love

You say: love は　にほんごで　なんと　いいますか。

You hear: love は　にほんごで　なんと　いいますか。

You repeat: love は　にほんごで　なんと　いいますか。

You hear: 「あい」と　いいます。

You write: <u>あい</u>

1. _____ 3. _____

2. _____ 4. _____

G. Matsuda-sensei says a word you don't understand. Ask for the meaning of the word. You will then hear the correct question. Repeat the question. You will then hear the answer to the question. Stop the tape and write the English word.

■ You hear: さかな

You say: 「さかな」って　なんですか。

You hear: 「さかな」って　なんですか。

You repeat: 「さかな」って　なんですか。

You hear: fish です。

You write: <u>fish</u>

1. _____ 4. _____

2. _____ 5. _____

3. _____ 6. _____

VI. Hiragana Small つ: Double consonants

A. Listen to each of the following pairs of words or phrases and identify which word or phrase in the pair has a double consonant. Circle first or second.

■ (first) second

1. first   second   5. first   second

2. first   second   6. first   second

3. first   second   7. first   second

4. first   second

B. Listen to each of the following pairs of words and identify each word that has a double consonant. Circle first, second, both, or neither.

■ first   second   both   (neither)

1. first   second   both   neither   4. first   second   both   neither

2. first   second   both   neither   5. first   second   both   neither

3. first   second   both   neither   6. first   second   both   neither

C. Listen to each of the following words or phrases first in English, then in Japanese. Repeat each of the Japanese words or phrases. You will then hear it again. Write each word or phrase. Stop the tape as necessary.

■ You hear: school, がっこう

You repeat: がっこう

You hear: がっこう

You write: がっこう

1. _____   4. _____

2. _____   5. _____

3. _____   6. _____

D. Listen to Professor Yamamoto's requests. Write the illustration number matching each request you hear.

■ <u>1</u>

   1   2   3   4   5

1. ____   5. ____

2. ____   6. ____

3. ____   7. ____

4. ____   8. ____

VII. Hiragana きゃ〜ぴょ:　Glides

A. Listen to each of the following pairs of words and identify which word in the pair has a glide. Circle first or second.

■ (first)　second

1. first　second
2. first　second
3. first　second

4. first　second
5. first　second
6. first　second

B. Listen to each of the following pairs of words and identify which words have a glide. Circle first, second, both, or neither.

■ first　(second)　both　neither

1. first　second　both　neither
2. first　second　both　neither
3. first　second　both　neither

4. first　second　both　neither
5. first　second　both　neither
6. first　second　both　neither

C. Listen to each of the following words or phrases first in English then in Japanese. Repeat each of the Japanese words or phrases. You will then hear it again. Write each word or phrase. Stop the tape as necessary.

■ You hear:　　homework,　しゅくだい

　You repeat:　しゅくだい

　You hear:　　しゅくだい

　You write:　しゅくだい

1. _____　　4. _____

2. _____　　5. _____

3. _____

D. A Japanese friend is speaking to you but you don't understand everything he says. Ask him to speak louder or slower or to repeat what he said, depending on what you hear. You will then hear the correct request. Repeat each request.

■ You hear:　　こんにちは。

　You say:　　ゆっくり　はなして　ください。

　You hear:　　ゆっくり　はなして　ください。

　You repeat:　ゆっくり　はなして　ください。

だいにか　(Chapter 2)
あいさつと　じこしょうかい
(Greetings and Introductions)

Part A - Pronunciation

Please turn to the Essential Vocabulary list on page 55 of your textbook and repeat each word or phrase you hear.

Part B - Speaking and listening comprehension activities

I. Identifying someone or something, using ～ は　～です

A. Look at the chart containing information about four people. Then listen to the following statements about them. Stop the tape. If a statement is true, write はい . If it is false, write いいえ .

■ <u>はい</u>

Name	さとう	もね モネ	きむ キム	ぶらうん ブラウン
Status	だいがくせい	だいがくせい	せんせい	がくせい
Nationality	あめりか アメリカじん	かなだ カナダじん	かんこくじん	お　すとらりあ オーストラリアじん
Year in school	さんねんせい	いちねんせい	N/A	だいがくいんせい

1. _____　　2. _____　　3. _____　　4. _____

5. _____　　6. _____　　7. _____　　8. _____

B. Look again at the chart in exercise A. You will hear a cue consisting of a name and nationality or a name and academic status or year in school. If the cue matches the information in the chart, respond to the cue orally, using ～は　～です. If the cue doesn't match the information in the chart, respond to the cue orally, using ～は　～じゃありません or ～は　～じゃないです. You will then hear the correct response. Write the correct response when you hear it.

■ You hear:　さとう// せんせい

　You say:　さとうさんは　せんせいじゃありません。

　or　　　　さとうさんは　せんせいじゃないです。

You hear: さとうさんは　せんせいじゃありません。

or 　　　　さとうさんは　せんせいじゃないです。

You write: <u>さとうさんは　せんせいじゃありません。</u>

or 　　　　<u>さとうさんは　せんせいじゃないです。</u>

1. _____

2. _____

3. _____

4. _____

5. _____

6. _____

7. _____

8. _____

II. Asking はい／いいえ questions, using ～は　～ですか

Using the following chart, answer each question orally. You will then hear the correct answer. Stop the tape and write the answer.

■ You hear: チョーさんは　せんせいですか。
　You say:　いいえ、そうじゃありません。
　or　　　　いいえ、そうじゃないです。
　You hear: いいえ、そうじゃありません。
　or　　　　いいえ、そうじゃないです。
　You write: いいえ、そうじゃありません。
　or　　　　いいえ、そうじゃないです。

Name	チョー	ロペス	スミス	ブラウン
Status	だいがくせい	だいがくせい	せんせい	がくせい
Nationality	ちゅうごくじん	メキシコじん	オーストラリアじん	アメリカじん
Year in school	いちねんせい	よねんせい	N/A	だいがくいんせい

1. _____

2. _____

3. _____

4. _____

5. _____

6. _____

7. _____

8. _____

III. Recognizing the relationship between nouns with の

A. Imagine that there are five scholars from Japan at your school this year. They are from different universities and teach different subjects. Listen to each statement about each scholar and university or subject and write the first **hiragana** of the scholar's name next to the appropriate university or subject. Stop the tape as necessary.

■ You hear: たなかせんせいの　だいがくは　とうきょうだいがくです。

　　You write: ___た___　とうきょうだいがく

Scholar	University	Subject
たなか	_____ とうきょうだいがく	_____ こうがく
やまだ	_____ わせだだいがく	_____ けいえいがく
きむら	_____ きょうとだいがく	_____ ぶんがく
いとう	_____ にほんだいがく	_____ かんこくご
おおき	_____ おおさかだいがく	_____ えいご

B. Look again at the chart in exercise A. Listen to each cue consisting of a university or a subject. Stop the tape and write a statement, using the noun の noun construction, identifying the scholar teaching that subject or at that university. You will then hear the correct answer. Verify your sentence.

■ You hear: とうきょうだいがく

You write: <u>たなかせんせいは　とうきょうだいがくの　せんせいです。</u>

You hear: たなかせんせいは　とうきょうだいがくの　せんせいです。

■ You hear: こうがく

You write: <u>やまだせんせいは　こうがくの　せんせいです。</u>

You hear: やまだせんせいは　こうがくの　せんせいです。

1. _____

2. _____

3. _____

4. _____

5. _____

6. _____

7. _____

8. _____

IV. Asking for personal information, using question words

Listen to the following questions about yourself and write your answers in Japanese. Stop the tape as necessary.

■ You hear: せんこうは　なんですか。

　　You write: <u>にほんごです。</u>

1. _____

2. _____

3. _____

4. _____

5. _____

V. Listing and describing similarities, using と and も

A. Look at the following chart. You will hear statements about the people in the chart. If the statement is true, write はい. If it is false, write いいえ. Stop the tape as necessary.

■ <u>はい</u>

Name	すみす スミスさん	ぶらうん ブラウンさん	り リーさん	もね モネさん
Nationality	あめりか アメリカじん	あめりか アメリカじん	かなだ カナダじん	かなだ カナダじん
Status	だいがくせい	だいがくいんせい	だいがくせい	だいがくいんせい
Major	あじあ アジアけんきゅう	こうがく	こうがく	あじあ アジアけんきゅう
University	UCLA	おおさかだいがく	UCLA	おおさかだいがく
Hometown	しかご シカゴ (Chicago)	しかご シカゴ	とろんと トロント (Toronto)	とろんと トロント

1. _____ 2. _____ 3. _____ 4. _____

5. _____ 6. _____ 7. _____ 8. _____

B. Look again at the chart in exercise A and listen to each statement about one of the people in the chart. Then, find the person who shares the same characteristic. Say a sentence using the particle も. You will then hear the correct response. Stop the tape and write the correct response.

■ You hear: すみす
スミスさんは　だいがくせいです。

You say: り
リーさんも　だいがくせいです。

You hear: り
リーさんも　だいがくせいです。

You write: <u>り
リーさんも　だいがくせいです。</u>

1. _____

2. _____

3. _____

4. _____

5. _____

6. _____

7. _____

8. _____

だいさんか　(Chapter 3)
にほんの　うち　(Japanese Houses)

Part A - Pronunciation

Please turn to the Essential Vocabulary list on page 85 of your textbook and repeat each word or phrase you hear.

Part B - Speaking and listening comprehension activities

I. Describing buildings and rooms, using adjective + noun

A. First look at the chart describing various buildings and places. Then listen to each of the following はい／いいえ questions and write はい or いいえ. Stop the tape as necessary.

■ You hear: たなかさんの　アパートは　きれいな　アパートですか。

You write: はい because Tanaka-san's apartment is pretty.

たなかさんの　アパート	きれい	ちいさい	しずか
だいがくの　りょう	ふるい	せまい	たかい
すずきさんの　うち	りっぱ	あたらしい	ちいさい
アリスさんの　へや	ひろい	あかるい	
じょうとうだいがく	おおきい	ゆうめい	いい

1. _____   3. _____   5. _____

2. _____   4. _____   6. _____

B. Listen to each of the following cues. Based on each cue, say a statement using adjective + noun. You will then hear the correct statement. Write each answer. Stop the tape as necessary.

■ You hear: わたしの　だいがく　／　ちいさい
You say: わたしの　だいがくは　ちいさい　だいがくです。
You hear: わたしの　だいがくは　ちいさい　だいがくです。
You write: わたしの　だいがくは　ちいさい　だいがくです。

1. _____

2. _____

3. _____

4. _____

5. _____

6. _____

II. Referring to places, things, and people, using この, その, あの, and どの

Look at the following drawing of a bedroom. You, Smith-san, are sitting on the bed (location A), and your friend is at location B. Listen to each of the following comments your friend makes about the room and its contents. If the location of each item is correctly indicated by what your friend says, circle はい; if it is not, circle いいえ.

■ (はい) いいえ

1. はい　いいえ	3. はい　いいえ	5. はい　いいえ
2. はい　いいえ	4. はい　いいえ	6. はい　いいえ

III. Describing the location of people and things, using 〜に　〜が　あります／います and ここ, そこ, あそこ

A. Look at the following drawing of a living-room. You, Smith-san, are sitting on the sofa (location A), and your friend is at location B. Listen to each of the following statements your friend makes about items in the room. If the location of each item is correctly indicated by what your friend says, circle はい; if it is not, circle いいえ.

■ (はい)　いいえ

1. はい　いいえ　　　3. はい　いいえ　　　5. はい　いいえ

2. はい　いいえ　　　4. はい　いいえ　　　6. はい　いいえ

B. Listen to each of the following questions and answer, first orally, then in writing. Stop the tape as necessary.

■ You hear: へやに　どんな　ものが　ありますか。

　You say : おおきい　つくえが　あります。

　You write: <u>おおきい　つくえが　あります。</u>

1. _____

2. _____

3. _____

4. _____

5. _____

6. _____

IV. Using location nouns: なか, そと, となり, よこ, ちかく, うしろ, まえ, うえ, した, みぎがわ, and ひだりがわ

Look at the following drawing of a bedroom and listen to each of the following conversations. If the information provided in the conversation is correct, write はい; if it is not, write いいえ.

■ いいえ

1. _____ 3. _____ 5. _____

2. _____ 4. _____ 6. _____

V. Using よ and ね

A. Listen to each of the following questions and answer it orally, using よ. Then stop the tape and write your answer.

■ You hear: がくせいですか。

You say: ええ、そうですよ。

You write: <u>ええ、そうですよ。</u>

1. _____

2. _____

3. _____

4. _____

5. _____

6. _____

B. Listen to each of the following questions and whenever possible, change the question into a statement, using ね. You will then hear the correct statement. Stop the tape and write each statement. If it is not possible to change the question, say "impossible."

■ You hear: がくせいですか。

You say : がくせいですね。

You hear: がくせいですね。

You write: <u>がくせいですね。</u>

■ You hear: あれは　なんですか。

You say: impossible

You hear: impossible

You write: <u>impossible</u>

1. _____

2. _____

3. _____

4. _____

5. _____

6. _____

だいよんか　(Chapter 4)
にほんの　まちと　だいがく
(Japanese Towns and Universities)

Part A - Pronunciation

Please turn to the Essential Vocabulary list on page 127 of your textbook and repeat each word or phrase you hear.

Part B - Speaking and listening comprehension activities

I. **Describing and commenting on places, using adjectives (polite affirmative and negative forms) and とても and あまり**

A. You will hear Lee-san talk about his university. After each statement, draw a line between the correct building or department and the adjective with which Lee-san describes it. If the statement is affirmative, write はい on the line to the right of the adjective; if it is negative, write いいえ. Stop the tape as necessary.

■ You hear: わたしの　だいがくは　とても　ふるいです。

だいがく	おおきい	_____
ラボ（らぼ）	あたらしい	_____
りょうの　へや	ふるい	____はい____
としょかん	たかい	_____
がくせいかいかん	ひろい	_____
たいいくかん	いい	_____
きょうようがくぶの　たてもの	ゆうめい	_____
こうがくぶの　たてもの	きれい	_____
	りっぱ	_____

B. Listen to each of the following questions and cues. Based on the cue, answer each question orally. You will then hear the correct answer. Repeat the answer.

- You hear: だいがくの　たてものは　おおきいですか。／　いいえ
  You say: いいえ、　おおきくありません。 or　おおきくないです。
  You hear: いいえ、　おおきくありません。 or　おおきくないです。
  You say: いいえ、　おおきくありません。 or　おおきくないです。

- You hear: だいがくの　たてものは　おおきいですか。／　ええ　とても
  You say: ええ、とても　おおきいです。
  You hear: ええ、とても　おおきいです。
  You say: ええ、とても　おおきいです。

II. Referring to things mentioned immediately before, using noun/adjective + の (pronoun)

In each of the following speeches or conversations, listen for adjective + の or noun + の. Write the expression. Also write what の refers to. Stop the tape as necessary.

■ <u>やまださんの</u>　<u>えんぴつ</u>

1. _____ _____   4. _____ _____

2. _____ _____   5. _____ _____

3. _____ _____

III. Referring to things, using これ, それ, あれ, and どれ

A. Look at the following drawing of a college campus. You and a friend are at locations A and B (in front of the student union). Listen to your friend's comments about the buildings on campus. If the location of each item is correctly indicated by what your friend says, circle はい; if it is not, circle いいえ.

■ ⟨はい⟩　いいえ

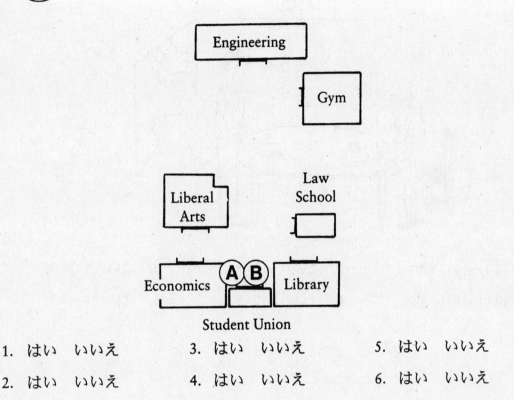

1. はい　いいえ
2. はい　いいえ
3. はい　いいえ
4. はい　いいえ
5. はい　いいえ
6. はい　いいえ

B. Look at the following drawing of a room. You are Tanaka-san, and Johnson-san is asking you how to say various objects in Japanese. Listen to each of her questions. If the location of each item is correctly indicated by Johnson-san's question, circle はい; if it is not, circle いいえ.

■ はい　⃝いいえ⃝

1. はい　いいえ　　　3. はい　いいえ　　　5. はい　いいえ

2. はい　いいえ　　　4. はい　いいえ　　　6. はい　いいえ

IV. Using は and が

Listen to each of the following incomplete questions and say a complete question, using は or が. You will then hear the correct question. Repeat each question.

■ You hear: だれ　せんせいですか。
　 You say: だれが　せんせいですか。
　 You hear: だれが　せんせいですか。
　 You say: だれが　せんせいですか。

V. Expressing location, using ～は　～に　あります／います and ～は　です

A. Look at the following picture of a street and listen to each of the following conversations. If the answer given in the conversation matches the picture, circle はい; if it does not match it, circle いいえ.

■ (はい)　いいえ

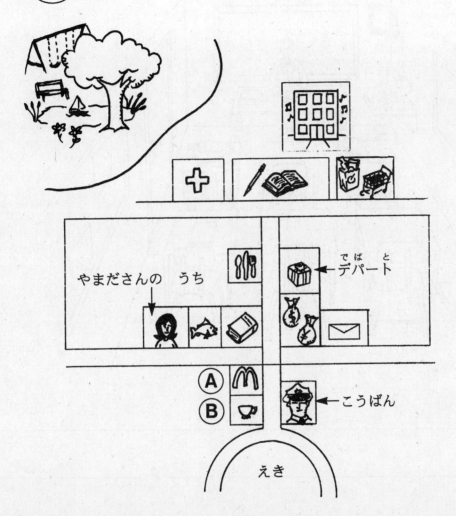

1. はい　いいえ　　　3. はい　いいえ　　　5. はい　いいえ

2. はい　いいえ　　　4. はい　いいえ

B. Look at the illustration of a classroom and listen to each of the following questions. Write the answer to each question, using a location noun and 〜は　〜に　あります／います or 〜は　〜です.

■　こくばんの　よこに　あります。　　or　　こくばんの　よこです。

1. _____

2. _____

3. _____

4. _____

5. _____

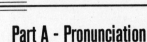

だいごか　(Chapter 5)
まいにちの　せいかつ　1
(Daily Routine 1)

Part A - Pronunciation

Please turn to the Essential Vocabulary list on page 157 of your textbook and repeat each word or phrase you hear.

Part B - Speaking and listening comprehension activities

I.　Telling time, using numbers, counters, and the particle に

A. Listen to each of the following time expressions and repeat it.

	〜じ (o'clock)	〜じかん(hours)	〜 ふん (minutes)
Question	なんじ	なんじかん	※なんぷん
1	いちじ	いちじかん	※いっぷん
2	にじ	にじかん	にふん
3	さんじ	さんじかん	※さんぷん
4	※よじ	※よじかん	よんふん／※よんぷん
5	ごじ	ごじかん	ごふん
6	ろくじ	ろくじかん	※ろっぷん
7	しちじ	しちじかん	しちふん／ななふん
8	はちじ	はちじかん	※はっぷん／はちふん
9	※くじ	※くじかん	きゅうふん
10	じゅうじ	じゅうじかん	※じゅっぷん／※じっぷん
11	じゅういちじ	じゅういちじかん	※じゅういっぷん
12	じゅうにじ	じゅうにじかん	じゅうにふん
20	にじゅうじ	にじゅうじかん	※にじゅっぷん／※にじっぷん
21	にじゅういちじ	にじゅういちじかん	※にじゅういっぷん

Note: ※ indicates a sound change.

B. Listen to the following time expressions. Write each time expression with arabic numerals.

■ 1:00 a. m.

1. _____ 3. _____ 5. _____ 7. _____ 9. _____

2. _____ 4. _____ 6. _____ 8. _____ 10. _____

C. Look at Yamada-san's schedule below. Listen to each of the following questions and answer it first orally, then in writing.

■ You hear: やまださんは　なんじに　おきますか。

  You say and write: しちじに　おきます。

7:00 a.m.	おきます。
7:30 a.m.	シャワーを　あびます。
8:10 a.m.	だいがくに　いきます。
8:30 a.m.	にほんごの　じゅぎょうが　はじまります。
9:20 a.m.	にほんごの　じゅぎょうが　おわります。
12:30 p.m.	ひるごはんを　たべます。
1:30 p.m.	ぶんがくの　じゅぎょうが　あります。
4:00 p.m.	うちに　かえります。

1. _____

2. _____

3. _____

4. _____

5. _____

6. _____

II. Telling what one does and where one does it, using the particles に, で, and を

A. Listen to each of the following incomplete sentences and say a complete sentence, using the correct particle. You will then hear the correct complete sentence.

■ You hear: テレビ みます

You say: テレビを みます。

You hear: テレビを みます。

B. Listen to each of the following incomplete questions and say a complete question, using the correct particle. You will then hear the complete question, followed by a cue. Answer the question, using the cue you hear, first orally, then in writing. You will then hear the correct answer.

■ You hear: なに よみます

You say: なにを よみますか。

You hear: なにを よみますか。／ ほん

You say and write: ほんを よみます。

You hear: ほんを よみます。

1. _____

2. _____

3. _____

4. _____

5. _____

6. _____

III. Expressing routines, future actions, or events, using the polite present forms of verbs

A. Look at Suzuki-san's schedule and listen to each of the following statements. If the statement is true, circle はい; if it is false, circle いいえ.

■ はい ⟨いいえ⟩

8:00 a.m.	wake up
8:30 a.m.	eat breakfast
9:15 a.m.	go to school
10:00 a.m.	class starts
11:50 a.m.	class ends
12:00 p.m.	eat lunch
1:30 p.m.	go to the library
4:00 p.m.	go home
6:30 p.m.	eat dinner
9:00 p.m.	take a bath
12:30 p.m.	go to bed

1. はい　いいえ　　　　3. はい　いいえ　　　　5. はい　いいえ

2. はい　いいえ　　　　4. はい　いいえ　　　　6. はい　いいえ

B. Look at Suzuki-san's schedule and answer each of the following questions, first orally then in writing, using はい、〜ます or いいえ、〜ません.

■ You hear: 　　　すずきさんは　はちじに　おきますか。

You say and write: <u>はい、おきます。</u>

1. _____　　4. _____

2. _____　　5. _____

3. _____　　6. _____

IV. Expressing frequency of actions, using adverbs

A. Listen to each of the following sentences, followed by an adverb of frequency. Say a new sentence, using the adverb provided and putting the verb in the appropriate form. You will then hear the correct sentence.

■ You hear: あさごはんを　たべます。　／　よく

You say: よく　あさごはんを　たべます。

You hear: よく　あさごはんを　たべます。

B. Listen to each of the following short conversations. After each conversation, draw lines to connect the appropriate name, activity, and frequency word.

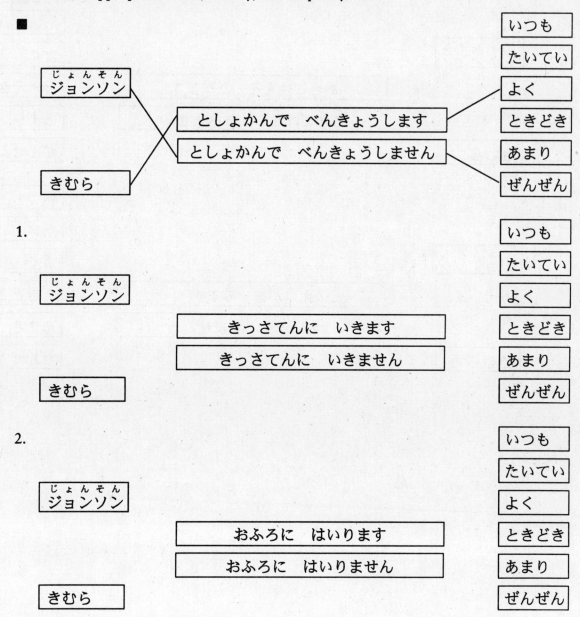

Laboratory Manual: Chapter 5   **237**

3.

ジョンソン

| コーヒーを　のみます |
| コーヒーを　のみません |

きむら

いつも
たいてい
よく
ときどき
あまり
ぜんぜん

4.

ジョンソン

| あさごはんを　たべます |
| あさごはんを　たべません |

きむら

いつも
たいてい
よく
ときどき
あまり
ぜんぜん

5.

ジョンソン

| えいがを　みます |
| えいがを　みません |

きむら

いつも
たいてい
よく
ときどき
あまり
ぜんぜん

V. Expressing approximate time and duration, using ごろ and ぐらい

A. Listen to each of the following time expressions and change it, using ごろ or ぐらい. You will then hear the correct response. Repeat the response.

- You hear: ごじ

  You say: ごじごろ

  You hear: ごじごろ

  You repeat: ごじごろ

B. Look at Tanaka-san's schedule. Tanaka-san is not very busy and his schedule is not rigid. Answer each of the following questions, using ごろ or ぐらい, first orally then in writing.

■ You hear:　　　　たなかさんは　なんじごろ　おきますか。

You say and write: <u>じゅうじごろ　おきます。</u>

～10:00 a.m.	wake up
～10:30 a.m.	eat breakfast
～12:30 p.m.	go to the library & study there
～2:20 p.m.	go to school
～3:00 p.m.	class starts
～4:20 p.m.	class ends
～4:30 p.m.	go to a friend's house
～6:00 p.m.	go home & eat dinner
～7:30 p.m.	watch TV
～10:00 p.m.	take a bath
～11:30 p.m.	go to bed

1. _____

2. _____

3. _____

4. _____

5. _____

6. _____

だいろっか　(Chapter 6)
まいにちの　せいかつ　2
(Daily Routine 2)

Part A - Pronunciation

Please turn to the Essential Vocabulary list on page 195 of your textbook and repeat each word or phrase you hear.

Part B - Speaking and listening comprehension activities

I. Expressing a means, using で; expressing starting and end points, using から～まで; expressing "to whom," using に; expressing "together with," using と

A. Listen to each of the following incomplete sentences and say a complete sentence, using the correct particle. You will then hear the correct complete sentence.

■　You hear:　　ともだち　／　でんわ　／　かけます

　　You say:　　ともだちに　でんわを　かけます。

　　You hear:　　ともだちに　でんわを　かけます。

　　You repeat:　ともだちに　でんわを　かけます。

B. Listen to each of the following conversations and answer each question in writing.

■　きょう　なんじに　だいがくに　きましたか。　　<u>はちじ</u>

1.　だれと　えいがを　みましたか。　　　　_____

2.　あしたの　しけんは　なんじまで　ありますか。　_____

3.　きょうは　なんで　だいがくに　きましたか。　　_____

4.　だれに　てがみを　よく　かきますか。　　　　_____

5.　だれと　レストランに　いきましたか。　　　　_____

II. Talking about past events, using polite past verbs and polite past adjectives

A. Listen to each of the following questions and cues. Answer each question orally, using the cue. You will then hear the correct answer.

■ You hear: きのう　しんぶんを　よみましたか。　／　いいえ

You say: いいえ、よみませんでした。

You hear: いいえ、よみませんでした。

B. Listen to each of the following questions and cues. Answer each question, using the cues. You will then hear the correct answer.

■ You hear: えいがは　どうでしたか。　／　あまり　／　おもしろい

You say: あまり　おもしろくありませんでした。

You hear: あまり　おもしろくありませんでした。

C. Listen to the following conversations. After each conversation, stop the tape and fill in the blank to complete each statement about the conversation.

■ おとこの　ひとは　きのう＿＿＿へやを　そうじしませんでした。

1. おとこの　ひとは　きのう ＿＿＿＿＿＿＿＿＿＿＿＿＿＿＿＿＿

2. しけんは ＿＿＿＿＿＿＿＿＿＿＿＿＿＿＿＿＿＿＿＿＿＿＿＿＿＿

3. おんなの　ひとは ＿＿＿＿＿＿＿＿＿＿＿＿＿＿＿＿＿＿＿＿＿

4. きのうの　えいがは　とても ＿＿＿＿＿＿＿＿＿＿＿＿＿＿＿＿

5. おんなの　ひとは　げつようびに ＿＿＿＿＿＿＿＿＿＿＿＿＿＿

III. Expressing frequency and extent, using counter expressions

A. Listen to each of the following statements and write in the blank in English the frequency, the extent, or the time frame of each action. Stop the tape as necessary.

■ _____once every two weeks_____

1. _____   4. _____

2. _____   5. _____

3. _____   6. _____

B. Look at the following schedule and listen to each of the following statements. If the statement is true, circle はい. If it is false, circle いいえ.

■ (はい)　いいえ

にち 日	げつ 月	か 火	すい 水	もく 木	きん 金	ど 土
30	1	2	3	4	5	6
てれび テレビ(3) れすとらん レストラン ともだちに てがみを かきます	にほんご(1) べんきょう(2) あるばいと アルバイト(2)	にほんご(1) けいざいがく (1.5) あるばいと アルバイト(2) ばんごはんを つくります ほんをよみ ます(1)	にほんご(1) べんきょう(2) ほんを よみます(1) ともだちに でんわを かけます	にほんご(1) けいざいがく (1.5) あるばいと アルバイト(2) ばんごはんを つくります てれび テレビ(2)	にほんご(1) うんどう(1) べんきょう(2) あるばいと アルバイト(2) てれび テレビ(2) ともだちに でんわを かけます	そうじを します せんたくを します えいがを みます ばんごはんを つくります

1. はい　いいえ　　　4. はい　いいえ　　　　7. はい　いいえ

2. はい　いいえ　　　5. はい　いいえ

3. はい　いいえ　　　6. はい　いいえ

IV. Using double particles with the topic marker は, the contrast marker は, and the similarity marker も

A. Listen to each of the following statements and, using the chart, complete each sentence, using は or も.

■ スミスさん <u>も</u> いそがしかったです。

	やまだ	すみす スミス	たなか
いそがしい	はい	はい	いいえ
ごはんを　つくります	いいえ	はい	はい
としょかんで　べんきょうします	はい	いいえ	はい
ひとりで　しゅくだいを　します	いいえ	いいえ	はい
じてんしゃで　きます	いいえ	はい	いいえ
ざっしを　かいます	はい	いいえ	いいえ

1. たなかさん_____

2. スミスさん_____
（すみす）

3. スミスさん_____
（すみす）

4. やまださん_____

5. たなかさん_____

6. たなかさん_____

B. Listen to each of the following conversations and complete each statement in writing. Stop the tape as necessary.

■ きのう　しごとを　しました。<u>でも、あしたは　しません。</u>

1. この　たてものは　としょかんです。_____

2. きのう　しんぶんを　よみました。_____

3. いっしゅうかんに　にどぐらい　うんどうを　します。_____

4. ひるごはんを　うちで　たべます。_____

Name _____ Class _____ Date _____

V. Expressing a reason, using 〜から, and expressing contrast, using が

A. Listen to each of the following short conversations. After each conversation, fill in the blank with the appropriate reason-giving sentence, using 〜から. Stop the tape as necessary.

■ （まいあさ）ジョギングを　しますから、ろくじに　おきます。

1. _____ でかけませんでした。

2. _____ しけんは　むずかしかったです。

3. _____ たいへんでした。

4. _____ がっこうに　きません。

B. Listen to each of the following short conversations. After each conversation, fill in the blank to complete each statement, using either 〜から or が, whichever is appropriate. Stop the tape as necessary.

■ あした　しけんが　ありますから、うちで　べんきょうします。

1. _____、りょうしんに　でんわを　かけませんでした。

2. _____、いぬは　いません。

3. _____、そうじを　しました。

4. _____、へやが　あまり　きれいじゃ　ありません。

5. _____、いい　ステレオを　かいました。

だいななか　(Chapter 7)
すきな　ことと　すきな　もの
(Activities and Hobbies)

Part A - Pronunciation

Please turn to the Essential Vocabulary list on page 238 of your textbook and repeat each word or phrase you hear.

Part B - Speaking and listening comprehension activities

I. Expressing likes and dislikes, using すき or きらい

A. Listen to each of the following speeches. After each speech, write what the person likes next to the smiling face and what the person dislikes next to the pouting face. Stop the tape as necessary.

■ ☺ _____テニス　　スキー_____

☹ _____ゴルフ_____

1. ☺ _____

☹ _____

2. ☺ _____

☹ _____

3. ☺ _____

☹ _____

4. ☺ _____

☹ _____

5. _____

    _____

B. Alice and Lee-san are talking in a restaurant. Listen to their conversation. After the conversation, look at each of the following statements. If a statement is true, circle はい; if it is false, circle いいえ.

■ (はい)　いいえ　　アリスさんは　やさいが　すきです。

1. はい　いいえ　　アリスさんは　コーヒーが　すきです。

2. はい　いいえ　　リーさんも　コーヒーが　すきです。

3. はい　いいえ　　アリスさんと　リーさんは　テニスが　すきです。

4. はい　いいえ　　アリスさんは　スキーが　あまり　すきじゃありません。

5. はい　いいえ　　リーさんは　スキーが　すきです。

6. はい　いいえ　　リーさんは　ゴルフは　あまり　すきじゃありません。

II. Making noun phrases, using の and the plain affirmative form of verbs (dictionary form)

A. Listen to each of the following verbs and say it in the plain present form. You will then hear the correct plain present verb. Write the verb.

■ You hear: あります
You say: ある
You hear: ある
You write: <u>ある</u>

1. _____ 6. _____ 11. _____

2. _____ 7. _____ 12. _____

3. _____ 8. _____ 13. _____

4. _____ 9. _____ 14. _____

5. _____ 10. _____ 15. _____

B. Listen to the following dialogues. After each dialogue, complete the statement by circling the correct choice. Stop the tape as necessary.

■ Ito-san likes _____

    a. cooking   b. bowling   (c.) reading   d. drinking

1. Smith-san likes _____ on weekends.

    a. playing basketball   b. swimming   c. walking   d. running

2. Kimura-san likes _____ in the park.

    a. sleeping   b. taking a walk   c. reading books   d. having lunch

3. Tanaka-san likes _____.

    a. playing baseball
    b. watching movies
    c. making movies
    d. watching baseball games

4. Brown-san dislikes _____.

    a. dancing   b. drinking sake   c. talking   d. singing

5. Ishida-san dislikes _____.

    a. going to movies   b. staying at home   c. exercising   d. going to concerts

III. Listing nouns, using や

Listen to each of the following dialogues with information about activities of the second speaker. Fill in the blank with either と or や, whichever is appropriate. Make your choice solely on the basis of the information given in the dialogues.

■ 田口さんは タイム＿と＿ ニューズウィークを よみます。

1. スミスさんは りょうしん＿＿＿ 日本の ともだちに よく てがみを

かきます。

2. 田中さんは コンサート＿＿＿ えいがに よく いきます。

3. 山田さんは 大学の しょくどう＿＿＿ きっさてんで よく ひるごはんを

たべます。

4. リーさんは としょかん＿＿＿ 学生 会館で よく べんきょうします。

IV. Making comparisons, using いちばん and 〜の　ほうが　〜より

A. Listen to each of the following questions. Choose the correct answer from the chart and write it on the line. Stop the tape as necessary.

■　<u>アラスカ</u>

ことばの　リスト
せかい　world
しゅう　state

<ruby>山<rt>やま</rt></ruby>	エベレスト<ruby>山<rt>ざん</rt></ruby> (Mt. Everest)	<ruby>富士山<rt>ふじさん</rt></ruby> (Mt. Fuji)	マッキンリー<ruby>山<rt>さん</rt></ruby> (Mt. McKinley)	
くに	バチカン	ロシア	ドイツ	フランス
しゅう (state)	アラスカ	ハワイ	ニューヨーク	カリフォルニア
まち	ニューヨーク	シカゴ	ロサンゼルス	

1. _____ 4. _____

2. _____ 5. _____

3. _____

B. Listen to each of the following questions and write your answer to each question. Stop the tape as necessary.

■　<u>さかなが　いちばん　すきです。</u>

1. _____

2. _____

3. _____

4. _____

5. _____

C. Listen to each of the following dialogues and circle the item to which the comparative adjective applies.

■ サンフランシスコ　（ロサンゼルス）

1. やきゅう　　フットボール

2. ビール　　ワイン

3. かんこく　　日本(にほん)

4. 日本語(にほんご)　　スペインご

5. ブラウンさんの　へや　　ホワイトさんの　へや

D. On the line that says "Your guess," write the name of each country, state, or city from the largest to the smallest. Then listen to the two comparative statements. After listening, stop the tape and write the name of each country, state, or city in the order specified by the comparative statements. Compare what you guessed and the order after listening.

■ イギリス　ドイツ　イタリア

Your guess: <u>ドイツ　イギリス　イタリア</u>

After listening: <u>ドイツ　イタリア　イギリス</u>

1. イタリア　　フランス　　日本(にほん)

Your guess: ＿＿＿＿＿＿＿＿　＿＿＿＿＿＿＿＿　＿＿＿＿＿＿＿＿

After listening: ＿＿＿＿＿＿＿＿　＿＿＿＿＿＿＿＿　＿＿＿＿＿＿＿＿

2. インディアナ　　アイオワ　　ニュージャージー

Your guess: ＿＿＿＿＿＿＿＿　＿＿＿＿＿＿＿＿　＿＿＿＿＿＿＿＿

After listening: ＿＿＿＿＿＿＿＿　＿＿＿＿＿＿＿＿　＿＿＿＿＿＿＿＿

3. とうきょう　　パリ　　ロンドン

Your guess: ＿＿＿＿＿＿＿＿　＿＿＿＿＿＿＿＿　＿＿＿＿＿＿＿＿

After listening: ＿＿＿＿＿＿＿＿　＿＿＿＿＿＿＿＿　＿＿＿＿＿＿＿＿

4. ニューヨーク　　シカゴ　　ロサンゼルス

Your guess: _____ _____ _____

After listening: _____ _____ _____

5. きょうと　　おおさか　　とうきょう

Your guess: _____ _____ _____

After listening: _____ _____ _____

V. Requesting and giving an explanation or a confirmation, using prenominal and plain present forms + んです

A. You have heard some rumors. Listen to each of the following statements and ask a confirmation question. You will then hear the correct question. Write the question.

■ You hear: アリスさんは　アメリカに　かえります。

　　You say:　アリスさんは　アメリカに　かえるんですか。

　　You hear: アリスさんは　アメリカに　かえるんですか。

　　You write: <u>アリスさんは　アメリカに　かえるんですか。</u>

1. _____

2. _____

3. _____

4. _____

5. _____

6. _____

7. _____

B. Listen to each of the following conversations and complete each sentence by supplying the correct reason. Stop the tape as necessary.

■ <u>さかなが　きらいです</u>から、たべません。

1. _____ から、大学(だいがく)に　きません。

2. _____ から、スーパーに　いきます。

3. _____ から、いきません。

4. _____ から、日本語(にほんご)を　べんきょうします。

5. _____ から、うちに　かえりません。

だい八か　(Chapter 8)
かいもの　(Shopping)

Part A - Pronunciation

Please turn to the Essential Vocabulary list on page 275 of your textbook and repeat each word or phrase you hear.

Part B - Speaking and listening comprehension activities

I. Making a request, using the て-form of a verb + 下^{くだ}さい

A. Listen to the following verbs in the dictionary form. Change each verb to its て-form and add 下^{くだ}さい. You will then hear the correct response. Repeat each response.

■　You hear:　みせる
　　You say:　　みせて下^{くだ}さい。
　　You hear:　みせて下^{くだ}さい。

B. Listen to each of the following conversations. After each conversation, look at the statement. If the statement is true, circle はい; if it is false, circle いいえ.

■　はい　（いいえ）　　Kim-san was speaking Japanese.

1. はい　いいえ　　Yamamoto-san wants to get the umbrella.

2. はい　いいえ　　The teacher wants to take a look at the book.

3. はい　いいえ　　The customer wants to have the watch put in a box.

4. はい　いいえ　　The customer wants to see a larger jacket.

　　　　Laboratory Manual: Chapter 8　　263

II. Using Chinese origin numbers, 100 and above

A. Listen to each of the following numbers while looking at the chart, and repeat each number.

Question	なんびゃく		なんせん		なんまん
100	ひゃく	1,000	せん	10,000	いちまん
200	にひゃく	2,000	にせん	20,000	にまん
300	※さんびゃく	3,000	※さんぜん	30,000	さんまん
400	よんひゃく	4,000	よんせん	40,000	よんまん
500	ごひゃく	5,000	ごせん	50,000	ごまん
600	※ろっぴゃく	6,000	ろくせん	60,000	ろくまん
700	ななひゃく	7,000	ななせん	70,000	ななまん
800	※はっぴゃく	8,000	※はっせん	80,000	はちまん
900	きゅうひゃく	9,000	きゅうせん	90,000	きゅうまん

Note: ※ indicates a sound change.

B. Listen to each of the following numbers and write it in arabic numerals.

■ 100

1. _____   8. _____   15. _____

2. _____   9. _____   16. _____

3. _____   10. _____   17. _____

4. _____   11. _____   18. _____

5. _____   12. _____   19. _____

6. _____   13. _____   20. _____

7. _____   14. _____

III. Referring to quantities with numbers and counters, using まい, 本, ひき, さつ, and Japanese origin numbers

A. Listen to each of the following numbers and counters while looking at the chart, and repeat each number and counter.

	Thin, flat objects	Long, cylindrical objects	Fish, small four-legged animals	Bound objects	Round, discrete objects
Counters	まい	ほん（本）	ひき	さつ	つ
Question	なんまい	※なんぼん	※なんびき	なんさつ	いくつ
1 （一）	いちまい	※いっぽん	※いっぴき	※いっさつ	ひとつ
2 （二）	にまい	にほん	にひき	にさつ	ふたつ
3 （三）	さんまい	※さんぼん	※さんびき	さんさつ	みっつ
4 （四）	よんまい	よんほん	よんひき	よんさつ	よっつ
5 （五）	ごまい	ごほん	ごひき	ごさつ	いつつ
6 （六）	ろくまい	※ろっぽん	※ろっぴき	ろくさつ	むっつ
7 （七）	ななまい	ななほん	ななひき	ななさつ	ななつ
8 （八）	はちまい	※はっぽん	※はっぴき	※はっさつ	やっつ
9 （九）	きゅうまい	きゅうほん	きゅうひき	きゅうさつ	ここのつ
10 （十）	じゅうまい	※じゅっぽん	※じゅっぴき	※じゅっさつ	とお

Note: ※ indicates a sound change.

B. Listen to each of the following conversations. Write each item mentioned and the quantity in arabic numerals.

■ <u>りんご</u>　　<u>3</u>

1. _____

2. _____

3. _____

4. _____

5. _____

IV. Referring to prices and floor levels, using 円 (えん) and かい

A. Listen to each of the following conversations. List each item mentioned and its price.

■ <u>本 (ほん)　￥2,500</u>

1. _____

2. _____

3. _____

4. _____

5. _____

B. You are in the elevator of a Japanese department store. Listen to what the elevator operator says and write the number of the floor on which you can buy each of the following items.

■ かばん　__1F__

1. ベッド　_____

2. ステレオ　_____

3. 本 (ほん)　_____

4. ワイン　_____

5. ドレス　_____

6. おとこの人の　コート　_____

7. スカート　_____

V. Abbreviating verbal expressions, using です

A. Listen to each of the following questions. If you can answer the question using です, circle はい; if you cannot, circle いいえ.

- ■ はい ⟨いいえ⟩

1. はい　いいえ　　　　4. はい　いいえ

2. はい　いいえ　　　　5. はい　いいえ

3. はい　いいえ　　　　6. はい　いいえ

B. Listen to each of the following questions and cues, and write your answer, using です.

- ■ <u>とけいです。</u>

1. _____　　4. _____

2. _____　　5. _____

3. _____

第九課 (Chapter 9)
レストランと しょうたい。
(Restaurants and Invitations)

Part A - Pronunciation

Please turn to the Essential Vocabulary list on page 311 of your textbook and repeat each word or phrase you hear.

Part B - Speaking and listening comprehension activities

I. Deciding on something, using 〜に　します, and making a request, using 〜を おねがいします

A. Listen to each of the following conversations. Write each item ordered.

■ <u>ラーメン</u>

1. _____ 4. _____

2. _____ 5. _____

3. _____

B. Listen to each of the following conversations. Write each item and quantity ordered.

■ <u>そば　1　うどん　2</u>

1. _____

2. _____

3. _____

II. Inviting and responding, using ～ませんか, ～ましょうか, and ～ましょう

A. Listen to each of the following dialogues. After each dialogue, choose from the box and write on the line the activity mentioned in the dialogue. If the person accepts the invitation, circle はい; if the person refuses, circle いいえ.

■ <u>えいがに いく</u>　(はい)　いいえ

うちに くる	ドライブを する	パーティを する
おちゃを のむ	でんしゃで いく	えいがに いく

1. _____ はい　いいえ

2. _____ はい　いいえ

3. _____ はい　いいえ

4. _____ はい　いいえ

5. _____ はい　いいえ

B. Listen to each of the following questions and cues and answer each question orally, using verb ましょう. You will then hear the correct answer. Repeat the answer.

■ You hear:　　どこに いきましょうか。(としょかん)

　　You say:　　としょかんに いきましょう。

　　You hear:　　としょかんに いきましょう。

　　You repeat:　としょかんに いきましょう。

C. Listen to each of the following conversations to grasp what the speakers are going to do and where they will do the activities being discussed. Write each activity and location. Stop the tape as necessary.

■ <u>すずきさんの うち で 山田さんの 誕生日^{たんじょうび} パーティーを します。</u>

1. _____

2. _____

3. _____

Laboratory Manual: Chapter 9 　275

III. Expressing purpose, using verb stem 〜に　いきます／きます／かえります

A. Listen to each of the following conversations and write in English each destination and purpose. Stop the tape as necessary.

- ■　スミス　　　　　<u>department store</u>　　<u>to buy shoes</u>

1. ジョンソン　　　_____　_____

2. リンダ　　　　　_____　_____

3. ジェーン　　　　_____　_____

4. キム　　　　　　_____　_____

B. Listen to each of the following conversations. After each conversation, write a sentence paraphrasing it. Make sure you include the destination and purpose. Use the names in the box.

- ■　この　人は　<u>ぎんざに　（トム　ハンクスの）えいがを　みに　いきます。</u>

Destinations	ぎんざ	ニューヨーク	アパート	うち	しんじゅく (in Tokyo)	らいらいけん (Name)

1. この　人は_____

2. この　人は_____

3. この　人は_____

4. この　人は_____

IV. Using a question word + か + (particle)

A. Listen to each of the following cues and ask a はい/いいえ question, using the particle か. You will then hear the correct question. Repeat each question.

■ You hear: きょうの　あさ　／　何（なに）　／　たべました

　You say: きょうの　あさ　何（なに）か　たべましたか。

　You hear: きょうの　あさ　何（なに）か　たべましたか。

　You repeat: きょうの　あさ　何（なに）か　たべましたか。

B. Listen to each of the following questions and answer each question first orally then in writing. Stop the tape as necessary.

■ You hear: きょうの　あさ　何（なに）か　たべましたか。

　You say and write: <u>はい、たべました</u>　or　<u>いいえ、たべませんでした。</u>

1. _____

2. _____

3. _____

4. _____

5. _____

Laboratory Manual: Chapter 9 279

V. Talking about activities and events, using ～で　～が　あります

Listen to each of the following statements. In response to each statement, ask a question about location. You will then hear the correct question, followed by the answer to the question. Write the answer on the line. Stop the tape as necessary.

■　<u>とけいが　つくえの　上に　あります。</u>

1. _____ あります。

2. _____ あります。

3. _____ あります。

4. _____ あります。

5. _____ あります。

6. _____ あります。

ききじょうず　はなしじょうず

Making and receiving telephone calls

A. You are making a telephone call to Yumiko Kinoshita at home in the evening. First listen to the conversation while looking at the following conversation template. Then play your role in the exchange. After each of your lines, stop the tape and write your line.

スミス :　_____。

だれか :　はい、そうです。

スミス :　_____、

　　　　　ゆみこさんは _____ か。

だれか :　はい、おります。　しょうしょう　おまち下さい。

Yumiko Kinoshita comes to the telephone.

ゆみこ :　もしもし、木下です。
　　　　　　　　　きのした

スミス :　_____

ゆみこ :　ああ　スミスさん、こんばんは。

B. You, Smith-san, receive three telephone calls. First listen to the example. Then say hello and respond to the person's greeting appropriately in each of the three short telephone conversations. After each conversation, stop the tape and write the name of the person calling you.

■　なまえ : すずきさん

1.　なまえ : _____

2.　なまえ : _____

3.　なまえ : _____

C. You, Smith-san, are making a telephone call to Hiroshi Katayama, at 473-5320, but you seem to have reached a wrong number. First listen to the conversation while looking at the following conversation template. Then play your role in the exchange. After each of your lines, stop the tape and write your line.

スミス： 　もしもし、_____ か。

だれか： 　いいえ、ちがいます。

スミス： 　あっ、_____ 。

　　　　　_____ か。

だれか： 　いいえ、ちがいますよ。４７３の　５０３２です。

スミス： 　_____

第十課 (Chapter 10)
だい か

私の家族 (My Family)
かぞく

Part A - Pronunciation

Please turn to the Essential Vocabulary list on page 349 of your textbook and repeat each word or phrase you hear.

Part B - Speaking and listening comprehension activities

I. Counting people, using 人; counting age, using さい; expressing the order within a family, using 番目.
にん / ばんめ

A. Listen to each of the following numbers and counters while looking at the chart, and repeat each number and counter.

	～人 (～ people) にん		～さい （～years old)		～番（目) (ordinal, ～th) ばん め	
何	なんにん	何人	なんさい	何さい	なんばん(め)	何番（目)
一	※ひとり	一人	※いっさい	一さい	いちばん(め)	一番（目)
二	※ふたり	二人	にさい	二さい	にばん(め)	二番（目)
三	さんにん	三人	さんさい	三さい	さんばん(め)	三番（目)
四	※よにん	四人	よんさい	四さい	よんばん(め)	四番（目)
五	ごにん	五人	ごさい	五さい	ごばん(め)	五番（目)
六	ろくにん	六人	ろくさい	六さい	ろくばん(め)	六番（目)
七	<u>しち</u>にん	七人	<u>なな</u>さい	七さい	<u>なな</u>ばん(め)	七番（目)
八	はちにん	八人	※はっさい	八さい	はちばん(め)	八番（目)
九	きゅうにん	九人	きゅうさい	九さい	きゅうばん(め)	九番（目)
十	じゅうにん	十人	※じゅっさい 十さい ※じっさい		じゅうばん(め)	十番（目)
百	ひゃくにん	百人	ひゃくさい	百さい	ひゃくばん(め)	百番（目)
千	せんにん	千人				
一万	いちまんにん	一万人				

Note: ※ indicates a sound change.

B. Look at the two family trees. You will hear a letter between A and T. Say the kinship term that corresponds with the letter. You will then hear the correct response. Repeat each response.

■ You hear: H

You say: 妹（いもうと）

You hear: 妹（いもうと）

You say: 妹（いもうと）

私の家族（かぞく）

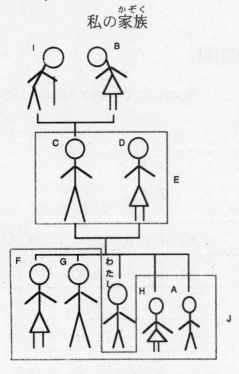

山田さんのご家族（かぞく）

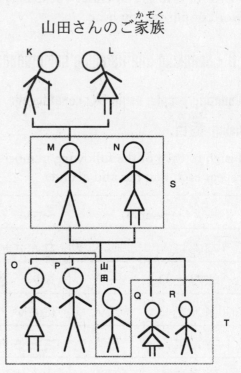

C. Look again at Yamada-san's family tree in exercise B. Answer each question in Japanese first orally then in writing. Write each number expression in **kanji** with **hiragana** super-script. Stop the tape as necessary.

■ You hear: ～さんは　何番目（なんばんめ）ですか。

You say and write: 上から　二番目（にばんめ）です。

1. _____

2. _____

3. _____

4. _____

5. _____

II. Describing a resultant state, using the verb て-form ＋ いる

A. Look at the drawings and listen to each of the following statements. If the statement is true, circle はい; if it is not, circle いいえ.

■ マクニールさんは　スーツを　きています。

(はい)　いいえ

マクニール
イギリス人
コンピュータの
かいしゃ

フランソワ
フランス人
モデル(model)

スコット
アメリカ人
大学生

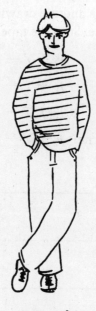

ルチアーノ
イタリア人
くつの　かいしゃ

コール
ドイツ人
大学院生
いん

ジャイシュリー
インド人
大学の先生

チャン
ちゅうごく人
大学生

リー
かんこく人
くるまの　かいしゃ

　　Laboratory Manual: Chapter 10　　287

1. はい　いいえ　　　　　4. はい　いいえ

2. はい　いいえ　　　　　5. はい　いいえ

3. はい　いいえ　　　　　6. はい　いいえ

B. Look again at the drawings in exercise A. Listen to each of the following cues and respond orally based on the cue and the drawings. You will then hear the correct response. Repeat then write the response. Stop the tape as necessary.

■ You hear:　　　　　　ルチアーノさん　／　めがね

　You say:　　　　　　ルチアーノさんは　めがねを　かけていません。

　You hear:　　　　　　ルチアーノさんは　めがねを　かけていません。

　You repeat and write: <u>ルチアーノさんは　めがねを　かけていません。</u>

1. _____

2. _____

3. _____

4. _____

5. _____

6. _____

III. Describing physical appearance and skills, using 〜は 〜が

A. Look again at the drawings in section II, activity A. Listen to each of the following statements. If the statement is true, circle はい; if it is false, circle いいえ.

■ スコットさんは　せが　たかいです。

(はい) いいえ

1. はい　いいえ　　　　　　4. はい　いいえ

2. はい　いいえ　　　　　　5. はい　いいえ

3. はい　いいえ　　　　　　6. はい　いいえ

B. Look again at the illustrations in section II, activity A. Listen to each of the following cues and say a sentence describing the person based on the cue. You will then hear the correct response. First repeat then write each response. Stop the tape as necessary.

■ You hear:　　　　　コールさん　／　かみ

　　You say:　　　　　コールさんは　かみが　みじかいです。

　　You hear:　　　　　コールさんは　かみが　みじかいです。

　　You repeat and write: <u>コールさんは　かみが　みじかいです。</u>

1. _____

2. _____

3. _____

4. _____

5. _____

6. _____

Laboratory Manual: Chapter 10

IV. Connecting phrases, using verb and adjective て-forms

A. Look again at the illustrations in section II, activity A. Listen to each of the following three descriptions and write the name of the person being described. Stop the tape as necessary.

■ <u>チャンさん</u>

1. _____

2. _____

3. _____

B. Listen to each of the following pairs of short sentences. Say a statement that combines the short sentences, using the て-form. You will then hear the correct statement. Repeat and then write each statement. Stop the tape as necessary.

■ You hear: やさしいです。 ／ きれいです。

You say: やさしくて きれいです。

You hear: やさしくて きれいです。

You repeat and write: <u>やさしくて きれいです。</u>

1. _____

2. _____

3. _____

4. _____

5. _____

V. Describing people and things, using nouns and modifying clauses

A. Look again at the illustrations in section II, activity A. Listen to each of the following statements. Decide who is the person described and write the appropriate sentence. Stop the tape as necessary.

■ <u>リーさんです。</u>

1. _____

2. _____

3. _____

4. _____

5. _____

6. _____

B. Look again at the illustrations in section II, activity A and listen to the following names. Describe first orally then in writing the people named, in terms of physical appearance, clothes, or possible skills and occupations, using nouns and modifier clauses. Stop the tape as necessary.

■ You hear: チャンさんと リーさん

You say and write: <u>口が　小さい人</u>
_{くち}

1. _____

2. _____

3. _____

4. _____

5. _____

第十一課 (Chapter 11)
だ い　か
おもいで　(Memories)

Part A - Pronunciation

Please turn to the Essential Vocabulary list on page 392 of your textbook and repeat each word or phrase you hear.

Part B - Speaking and listening comprehension activities

I. **Talking about time, using noun/adjective +** 時 とき, ～月 がつ, ～日 にち, ～か月 げつ, **and duration+** まえ(に)

A. Listen to each of the following time expressions for months and days while looking at the chart, and repeat each time expression.

1. Months of the year:

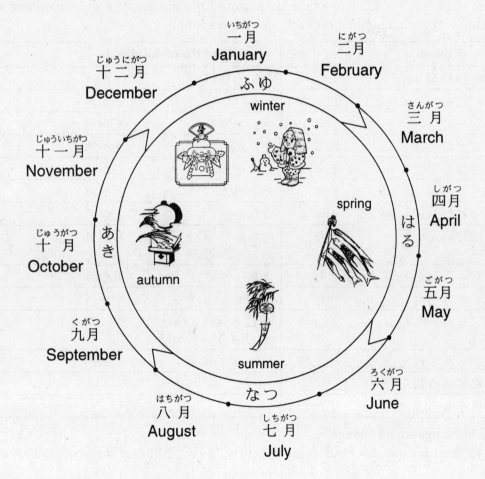

2. Days of the month:

日	月	火	水	木	金	土
		一日 ついたち*	二日 ふつか	三日 みっか	四日 よっか	五日 いつか
六日 むいか	七日 なのか	八日 ようか	九日 ここのか	十日 とおか	十一日 じゅういち にち	十二日 じゅうに にち
十三日 じゅう さんにち	十四日 じゅう よっか	十五日 じゅうご にち	十六日 じゅうろく にち	十七日 じゅうしち にち	十八日 じゅうはち にち	十九日 じゅうく にち
二十日 はつか	二十一日 にじゅう いちにち	二十二日 にじゅう ににち	二十三日 にじゅう さんにち	二十四日 にじゅう よっか	二十五日 にじゅう ごにち	二十六日 にじゅう ろくにち
二十七日 にじゅう しちにち	二十八日 にじゅう はちにち	二十九日 にじゅう くにち	三十日 さんじゅう にち	三十一日 さんじゅう いちにち		

B. Listen to each of the following time expressions for duration in years and months while looking at the chart, and repeat each time expression.

	～年 (year)		～か月 (months of duration)	
1	いちねん	一年	※いっかげつ	一か月
2	にねん	二年	にかげつ	二か月
3	さんねん	三年	さんかげつ	三か月
4	※よねん	四年	よんかげつ	四か月
5	ごねん	五年	ごかげつ	五か月
6	ろくねん	六年	※ろっかげつ	六か月 （はんとし　半年）
7	ななねん／しちねん	七年	ななかげつ	七か月
8	はちねん	八年	はちかげつ or ※はっかげつ	八か月
9	きゅうねん or くねん	九年	きゅうかげつ	九か月
10	じゅうねん	十年	※じゅっかげつ	十か月
11	じゅういちねん	十一年	※じゅういっかげつ or じゅういちかげつ	十一か月
12	じゅうにねん	十二年	じゅうにかげつ	十二か月
20	にじゅうねん	二十年		
24	にじゅうよねん	二十四年		

Note: ※ indicates sound change.

*いちにち means *one day* for duration whereas ついたち means *the first day of the month*.

Name _____ Class _____ Date _____

C. Listen to each of the following dialogues and write in arabic numerals the time expression you hear.

■ <u>8 o'clock</u>

1. _____   4. _____   7. _____

2. _____   5. _____   8. _____

3. _____   6. _____

Laboratory Manual: Chapter 11

II. Talking about past experiences, using verb たことがある; listing representative activities, using verb たり verb たりする

A. Listen to each of the following verbs and say it in the plain past affirmative form. You will then hear the correct response.

- ■ You hear: たべる

  You say: たべた

  You hear: たべた

B. Listen to each of the following dialogues, followed by a question. Write はい or いいえ based on what you heard. Stop the tape as necessary.

- ■ <u>いいえ</u>

1. _____ 4. _____

2. _____ 5. _____

3. _____ 6. _____

C. You are an administrator of an elementary school and are looking for a teacher who speaks English fluently and likes small children and sports. Listen to the interviews of four candidates. Stop the tape whenever necessary to take notes in English. After listening to the interviews, write the name of the person whom you consider to be the best candidate.

	えいご	子供	スポーツ
やまだ 山田さん			
やまもと 山本さん			
かわかみ 川上さん			
たぐち 田口さん			

一番 いい人は_____です。

III. Expressing reasons, using the plain past form of verbs and adjectives +んです and the plain form of verbs and adjectives + からです

A. Listen to each of the following expressions and change it to the plain form. You will then hear the correct response. Repeat and then write the correct response.

■ You hear: おもしろいです

You say: おもしろい

You hear: おもしろい

You repeat and write: <u>おもしろい</u>

1. _____   7. _____

2. _____   8. _____

3. _____   9. _____

4. _____   10. _____

5. _____   11. _____

6. _____   12. _____

B. Listen to each of the following dialogues. Complete each incomplete sentence by writing the correct reason, using ～からです. Stop the tape as necessary.

■ 田中さんは 家に 帰りました。<u>しけんの べんきょうが あった</u>
からです。

1. きょうとに 行きました。＿＿＿＿＿＿＿＿＿＿＿＿＿＿＿＿ からです。

2. 山に のぼるのは すきじゃありません。＿＿＿＿＿＿＿＿＿ からです。

3. ジャケットを きていません。 ＿＿＿＿＿＿＿＿＿＿＿＿＿ からです。

4. コートを 買いました。 ＿＿＿＿＿＿＿＿＿＿＿＿＿＿＿ からです。

5. あした びょういんに 行きます。 ＿＿＿＿＿＿＿＿＿＿＿ からです。

IV. Expressing hearsay, using the plain form of verbs, adjectives, the copula +そうです

Listen to each of the following conversations and complete each sentence in writing, using そうです. Stop the tape as necessary.

■ 山田さんは　しゃしんを　とりに　山に　行ったそうです。

1. スミスさんは _____。

2. 田中さんは _____。

3. 川上さんは _____。

4. ブラウンさんは _____。

5. キムさんは _____。

6. 川口さんは _____。

V. Using noun-modifying clauses in the past and present

A. Listen to each of the following dialogues then look at the statement. If the statement is true, circle はい; if it is false, circle いいえ.

■ (はい) いいえ きのう おいしい おすしを 食べました。

1. はい　いいえ　山田さんは　富士山に　のぼりました。

2. はい　いいえ　田中さんは　子供の時　よく　あそびました。

3. はい　いいえ　スミスさんは　リーさんが　すきでした。

4. はい　いいえ　川上さんは　学校の　うしろに　ある　こうえんに　よく　行きます。

5. はい　いいえ　大木さんは　さむい　ところが　すきです。

6. はい　いいえ　山本さんは　きのう　じゅぎょうに　来ました。

B. Listen to each of the following dialogues. After each dialogue, write what kinds of things or people are being discussed, using nouns and modifying clauses.

■ えいごが　上手な　人

1. _____

2. _____

3. _____

4. _____

5. _____

6. _____

第十二課　(Chapter 12)
だい　　か
健康　(Health)
けんこう

Part A - Pronunciation

Please turn to the Essential Vocabulary list on page 425 of your textbook and repeat each word or phrase you hear.

Part B - Speaking and listening comprehension activities

I. Expressing capability, using the potential forms of verbs

A. Listen to each of the following verbs and say the present potential form. You will then hear the correct response. Repeat and then write the correct response. Stop the tape as necessary.

■ You hear:　　　　　　　あるく

　You say:　　　　　　　あるける　あるけない

　You hear:　　　　　　　あるける　あるけない

　You repeat and write: <u>あるける　あるけない</u>

1. _____　　5. _____

2. _____　　6. _____

3. _____　　7. _____

4. _____　　8. _____

B. Listen to each of the following questions in Japanese and write your answer. Stop the tape as necessary.

■ You hear:　どんな　スポーツが　できますか。

　You write: <u>テニスや　スキーが　できます。</u>

1. _____

2. _____

　　　　Laboratory Manual: Chapter 12　　307

3. _____

4. _____

5. _____

6. _____

II. Expressing cause, using the て-form of adjectives and verbs

Listen to each of the following dialogues then read the question. Write your answer to each question. Stop the tape as necessary.

■ どうして 金田さんの かおは あかいんですか。

　　ねつが あるからです。　or　ねつが あるんです。

1. 木村さんは どうして 薬を 飲むんですか。

_____

2. どうして 目が かゆいんですか。

_____

3. 男の人は どうして 「いたい」と いいましたか。(Why did the man say "いたい"?)

_____

4. 女の人は どうして はなが つまっているんですか。

_____

5. さとうさんは どうして しごとを 休んだんですか。

_____

III. Expressing desire, using verb stem + たい and たがる

A. Listen to each of the following conversations and circle the choice that fits the content of the conversation.

■ The man wants (to eat steak / to cook steak).

1. The man (wants / does not want) to go out.

2. The man wants (to climb a mountain / to go to Kyoto).

3. The woman wants (to eat good food / to have a party).

4. The woman wants (to play tennis / to see a movie).

5. The man wants to drink (juice / an alcoholic beverage).

B. Listen to each of the following questions and write your answer.

■ <u>テニスが　したいです。</u>

1. _____

2. _____

3. _____

4. _____

5. _____

6. _____

IV. Giving suggestions, using 〜たら　どうですか and 〜ほうが　いいです

A. Listen to each of the following conversations and look at the statement. If the statement is true, circle はい; if it is false, circle いいえ.

- ■　(はい)　いいえ　　The woman suggests that the man go home.

1.　はい　いいえ　　The woman suggests that the man drink some water.

2.　はい　いいえ　　The woman warns the man not to smoke cigarettes.

3.　はい　いいえ　　The woman suggests that the man take a rest.

4.　はい　いいえ　　The man suggests that the woman eat meat.

5.　はい　いいえ　　The man suggests that the woman put on a bandage.

6.　はい　いいえ　　The man suggests that the woman wear a coat.

B. Listen to each of the following suggestions and write one possible situation for each suggestion.

- ■　おなかが　いたい　　or　　ふとっている

1. _____

2. _____

3. _____

4. _____

5. _____

6. _____

7. _____

8. _____

V. Asking for and giving permission, using verb stem + てもいいですか

A. Listen to each of the following conversations. Each conversation is numbered and contains a request. Look at the request topics below and after you hear each conversation, identify the request you heard with the conversation number. Then if the request is granted, circle はい; if it is not granted, circle いいえ. Stop the tape as necessary.

■ ___1___   たばこを　すう　　　　はい　(いいえ)

_____   じゅぎょうを　休^{やす}む　　はい　いいえ

_____   おすしを　食^たべる　　はい　いいえ

_____   おさけを　飲^のむ　　　はい　いいえ

_____   くるまで　行^いく　　　はい　いいえ

_____   ひとり　行^いく　　　はい　いいえ

B. You will hear a series of cues. After each cue, say a question that asks for permission. You will then hear the correct question. Write the question.

■ You hear:　ここで　ねる

　　You say:　　ここで　ねても　いいですか。

　　You hear:　ここで　ねても　いいですか。

　　or　　　　ここで　ねても　いいでしょうか。

　　or　　　　ここで　ねても　かまいませんか。

　　You write:　<u>ここで　ねても　いいですか。</u>

　　or　　　　<u>ここで　ねても　いいでしょうか。</u>

　　or　　　　<u>ここで　ねても　かまいませんか。</u>

1. _____

2. _____

3. _____

4. _____

5. _____

6. _____